The Super Star
In YOU!

Richard Söderblom

Although the author and publisher have made every effort to ensure that the information in this book was correct at press time, the author and publisher do not assume and hereby disclaim any liability to any party for any loss, damage, or disruption caused by errors or omissions, whether such errors or omissions result from negligence, accident, or any other cause.

First Publication: December 2013

ISBN: 1492269131
ISBN-13: 978-1492269137

http://www.coachingwithrichard.com

DEDICATION

This book, "The Super Star In YOU!", is dedicated to my wife, Lucinda Söderblom, who has stood by my side and supported me through all the long hours in assembling this book.

I want to thank my lovely children for simply being the best that they possibly can and making me the proudest father in existence.

I also want to thank you, the reader, for picking up this book and taking the time to read and learn the principles taught in it, so that you may grow and become more productive and valuable and become the Super Star that you are meant to be.

THANK YOU

CONTENTS

ACKNOWLEDGMENTS

I would like to acknowledge Michael Sliwinski who provided the basis for the productivity system I use and teach to my clients.

FOREWORD

Being a property investor, speaker, mentor and author keeps me extremely busy. Due to a very busy schedule I need to be on-top of my game. Managing over 250 properties successfully means that I need to be really productive and make the time I spend during the day count.

To help me be on peak performance at all times means I need to have the right productivity tools that will work for me and make me more efficient and effective.

Richard Söderblom wrote this book with the person in mind that is struggling to cope, constantly tired, lacking motivation and morale, and I believe that he hit the proverbial nail on the head with this book.

Richard explores and divulges some of the productivity tools and techniques that I have been using for years to be successful and stay ahead of the pack. He goes into the details of how to use these techniques and tools in your life right away.

The book is written in easy to understand language and is certainly one of the best that I have read on this topic.

A must read for you if you are in need to up your game, increase your productivity and improve your performance.

This book will change your life!

Gordon Mackay
www.gordonmackay.co.za

INTRODUCTION

Thank you for purchasing this book. You have taken one of the best possible steps you could to increasing your knowledge. If you implement the tips, techniques and strategies that are discussed in this book, not only will you become more productive at what you do, but you will have increased your value to your clients, your boss, yourself, immensely.

In today's world, there is a greater abundance of opportunity for both organizations and individuals to accomplish extraordinary goals. However, all too often, the demands of our jobs, coupled with the barrage of information coming at us from so many sources (e.g. texts, emails, reports, tweets, blogs, web-sites, etc.) is overwhelming, exhausting and distracting. The sheer volume of distractions threatens our ability to think clearly and make good decisions. If we react to these stimuli without careful discernment, we will sink into a sea of irrelevancy and fail to accomplish the things that matter most in our professional and personal lives.

When we deliberately pay attention to the most important things amidst the distractions, we can harness the opportunities and technologies available today and soar to creative and innovative heights.

What we will look at in this book, is of course, how to be more productive! ☺

Managing your time and productivity is, well, not a 'sexy' topic. No matter how I try, I cannot put a big spin on it. It is a silent success system, so I can't put much 'hype' into it.

It is simple though. The people who can produce the most work and make the most of their time can make **more** money in **less** time.

Being productive consists of doing various things that tie in together and doing them well. Leave one piece out and overall productivity suffers.

We will cover how to set goals correctly, using probably the most brilliant method ever devised. We will look at how to cure procrastination forever. This is probably one of the biggest opponents to being productive. We will look at how to become energized and of course see how we can be more productive by implementing some easy methods that will up the results we achieve at the end of the day.

While the techniques and methods shown here work wonders for me, I encourage you to take these concepts and experiment with them. Find what works best for you. The concepts we will discuss here are phenomenally powerful, however we are all different and what works for some people may not necessarily work as well for others.

Therefore take these methods and systems and use them as the basis for your own unique and individual style. You can only win.

"Nothing is so fatiguing as the
eternal hanging on of an
uncompleted task." – William James

1: MOTIVATING YOURSELF

In order to be able to complete a task satisfactorily takes a certain amount of motivation. Besides having the necessary skill and knowledge about the said task this element of motivation is what is going to keep the individual on track.

What Does It Mean To Be Motivated

Self-motivation is probable the single most important element in keeping an individual interested and committed to finishing a set task.

The doubt factor that is always present in every scenario requires some level of motivation in order to ensure the doubt is kept in check or at bay. In life it is not always possible to only do things or be exposed to things that only bring pleasure.

There will be times when some discipline is required to get through a task even if it is uncomfortable and displeasure able, and here is where one needs to be self-motivated.

The Basics

Some of the things that may help an individual to stay motivated are as follows:

> ➤ Keeping the end goal in clear focus. When the end goal is clearly imprinted in the mind's eye, then the body and mind will be able to subconsciously condition themselves to suit the needs of the individual to successfully complete the task set.

> ➤ Continuously reminding one's self of the capabilities and the conviction that it is possible to finish the task. This continual reminder will then translate into a zest and even the chemical reaction within the body and mind that produces the extra energy to keep going.

> ➤ Stepping back and viewing the task in its present percentage of accomplishment will also help to create a further motivational level to complete it. This is more so when the physical accomplishment to that point is on the positive side.

> ➤ Facilitating little rewards to be enjoyed as each level in the task is achieved can also be a good motivational tool.

Understand Yourself And Where You Need Work

Most people just try to get through each day without really learning to appreciate it for all it has to offer. More so in today's fast pace world there is really very little opportunity to stop and think let alone indulge in something that may really be enjoyable to pursue. There is always the thought that "I will do it someday." Sometime however there is a need to stop and take stock of one's life to ensure the zest for living is still very much alive and well.

Important Info

In the process of taking a clear and serious look at one's life to date, several different questions should be asked and addressed in order to help the individual lead a more fruitful and motivated daily life. In pursing this, the individual will then be able to find happiness and contentment as the motivation levels will be higher than ever.

Having a goal in life that is both rewarding and achievable in the eye of the individual is what is going to keep the said individual on track and in success. Doing something that really brings joy and peace should not really be considered a privilege as it is possible to work towards finding something that brings on these positive feelings with a little focused understanding of one's self.

When this is clearly understood, the mind and the body will work together to make the circumstances possible to achieve anything desired. The inspiration needed to carry the mind set to completing the task will be the dominating factor.

Being able to identify what area of activities most benefits and excites the individual is also another advantage worth exploring. When one is excited about something there is very little need to push it to success.

Keep A Positive Mindset

Positive people are not only a joy to be around but they are also the people that get things done. Mostly they get whatever they work towards because of the motivation they utilize in order to always look at things from a positive mind set.

Altering Thinking

There are several ways to keep the negative elements or mind set away and from possibly causing problems from within. Here are some thoughts on the matter:

> ➢ Always try to stay calm in every situation. Panic does not help and can even cause irrevocable changes.

> ➢ Forcing one's self to keep a gentle tone will in turn force the body chemical to react better to the situation and thus work towards causing the mind to slowly calm down and relax.

- ➤ Always make it a habit to look for as many positive elements as possible in any given negative situation. When one constantly trains to look for the positive, the chances of letting the situation overwhelm and cause other negative vibes can be controlled successfully.

- ➤ Being around people who are equally positive will always prove to be a wise choice indeed. Positive people focus on staying positive no matter what the situation is, as opposed to being only able to stir up negative points.

- ➤ Coming to the realization that constantly taking the negative stand will only bring deeper and larger problems should be enough of a reason to start being positive.

- ➤ Learning from mistakes is sometimes the best way to move forward. This gives the individual a chance to exercise skills perhaps unknown or buried deep within. It can also be very satisfying when the negative is turned into a positive.

- ➤ Listening to positive motivational messages and talking to people who advocate a constant positive mindset is also encouraged. The tips they impart can be invaluable.

Associate With Positive People

As previously mentioned there are a lot of merits in ensuring a positive mindset. Therefore going a step further and making the conscious effort to surround yourself with positive people always will in fact be the best formula to follow.

Positive

If you are seriously interested in becoming a better person, the first wise step to make is to ensure those within the inner circle in your life or those in constant contact with you are always of the positive nature.

The general wisdom behind this thinking is that whatever positive practices and value held by these positive minded associates will eventually be copied and practiced by you too.

Negative people always find reasons to drag themselves and those around them down. Perhaps it is because they are more comfortable if everyone else is miserable too.

However positive people will take the time and effort to impart or impact as many positive values as they can to someone who is interested in achieving the same positive outlook in life as them.

Among the positive characteristics of positive people are the ability to be enthusiastic about almost anything, an uncanny zest for life, a willingness to try anything, cheerful, inspired are just a few to name. All these character traits are very enticing to be a part of and if an individual is open to being led then it is possible to learn to look at things through the eyes of these positive people and thus really begin to enjoy life.

Associating with positive people whenever the opportunity presents itself is also beneficial intellectually and in building stronger character traits. Positive people tend to be well informed and in the know always. They usually make a conscious effort to keep up with the latest in everything.

Put Your Goals Where You Can See It

In order to see a task to completion and with the same motivational levels as at the beginning of the task, it would be prudent to have the goal expected to be derived from the task to be as visible as possible. This not only applies to having this goal firmly imprinted in the mind's eye but also should be physically visible as much as possible.

Look At It

If the goal is not only foremost in your thoughts but also "around" you, then the battle to keep the task featured as a constant and important factor daily is achieved. Many people advocate the physical presence of the goal help to keep them focused until the end desired results are achieved.

Some of the ways that can be used successfully are putting up visual aids that depict the desired goal. Others may include keeping a log book of sorts to chart the progress made towards achieving the goal. There are some people that go as far as to have a replica of what they want to achieve made. The idea really is to keep the goal as visible as possible through any means available in order to keep the motivation levels as high and as constant as possible.

If the goal in question can be successfully broken up into different stages then keeping a chart that visibly tracks the progress of the task toward the end achievement, helps to create the necessary satisfaction levels within yourself in the visibility of the progress at hand. The nearer the end becomes visible the more the adrenaline levels will rise and thus produce more energy and zest to see the task perhaps achieved at a quicker pace. Getting friends to help keep track of the progress with you also helps to keep the goal in focus.

Reward Yourself For Small Advancements

Rewards are always a wonderful thing to receive especially if the efforts put into a task to achieve the rewards has been quite monumental. Rewards are also a great way to keep motivated and focus on the task to see it to completion.

Praise

Breaking a task into sections has many merits one of which is it allows you or those involved in the task process to be able to physically see the progress and monitor it accordingly.

This also creates the opportunity to pass out little rewards when each stage is achieved. These rewards are a great incentive to ensure those involved in the task are able to stay focus and totally committed to seeing the said task to successful completion.

However the types of rewards and the methods linked to meriting the rewards should be carefully considered lest it turn out to have adverse effects instead.

Drawing up a system that charts the progress and associates the different stages to different rewards given out should be done early on in the project frame work. The rewards chosen should match the progress made.

Choosing the right rewards is very important as it is supposed to act as an incentive and the wrong array of rewards may not cause those involved to be motivated but instead cause them to doubt their contribution values to the success of the project. This can indeed have very damaging result on the morale and general attitude towards keeping up the motivation to succeed.

Rewards that are tailored to bring on the excitement and satisfaction when a certain level in the project is reached will not only cause the added zest needed it will also contribute to you working harder to achieve the next level of advancement in order to be rewarded again. This new found added zest is very beneficial as these spurts of energy also bring new life into the project at every few stages.

Don't Forget To Get Excited

Staying excited is a very important tool to ensure the mindset does not give up half way during the project started. This will not only be a bad habit to pick up it will also cause detrimental effects in the long run.

Energize

The excitement factor will always be able to motivate you to keep moving forward toward achieving the goals set. This key ingredient is what attracts people to consider or embark on a project. Those who stay excited have the positive mindset that is required and also necessary to ensure the success of any project or endeavor.

Sharing the ideas in the intended project with others helps to keep the excitement levels high. When a person is passionate about their endeavors it shows clearly in the way they talk about the project.

This excitement more often than not carries over to the others listening. There are even scientific researches done that attest to the proven facts that there are a lot of positive chemical changes that happen in the body system when the excitement levels are apparent.

Setting time lines and dates at every juncture of the project has its benefits is keeping the excitement levels high. Whenever these time lines or deal lines are successfully met you or your group experiences another level of satisfaction which in turn creates the positive element of excitement.

Believing strongly in the project is also another way to keep being excited about the project. If the belief is strong then any and all negative encounters along the way can be easily overcome because of the excitement levels that can counter these setbacks that may occur from time to time. Most people who passionately believe in themselves and their abilities to successfully achieve anything are usually very well balanced and success orientated people.

Learn To Be Dedicated

Dedication is also another prerequisite to being able to achieve many things impossible or otherwise. It is often one of the most important factors needed to be in place and evident even before a project is embarked upon.

Stay Focused

Some of the ways to stay as dedicated as possible are as follows:

> ➤ Having a love for what is required in terms of work processes in the project is important. Those people who tend to focus on the end goal rather than what it takes to get there, soon find out that they are in a rather unhappy and stressful journey. This then shifts the dedication commitment levels which can cause serious problems and effects to the project in question.

> ➤ Being dedicated is also being persistent. If the persistency element is evident then the individual is able

to work hard and do whatever is required in order to complete any endeavor started.

➤ Keeping to a suitable and workable routine is also helpful as it shows the level of dedication involved. This not only helps the mindset but also allows the body to condition itself to work towards achieving the goal set.

➤ When the object of the goal brings a certain level of personal gratification and at the same time is also for the good of others the dedication levels an individual is prepared to extend can be phenomenal.

➤ Seeking help along the way may also show that the individual is very committed to completing the task. When faced with a problem that requires the expertise that the individual does not have, seeking outside help is one way of staying true to the project and maintaining the dedication levels.

➤ Being able to move forward when mistakes are made also requires a certain dedication level. The dedication levels evident will dictate the lengths the individual is willing to go in order to achieve success

Get Support From Others If Necessary

Standing alone is never a good idea when trying to achieve something. Everyone needs friends and family to provide the necessary encouragement and help that is sometimes required to see any endeavor to its successful end.

Some Suggestions

The support and encouragement from other can have very far reaching and powerful effects. These elements play a huge part in helping you keep up the zest, will or discipline to succeed.

Another reason it is important to have outside support is that sometime those not immediately connected to the project or endeavor can see more clearly the situation and make the helpful comments and give helpful advice. This is indeed invaluable to you if you are stuck in a rut and unable to see a way out.

Being open to accepting support can also create the circumstances for new relationships or opportunities to present itself. These can bring about a more fruitful and positive outcome and perhaps even a new positive light to the whole project. Closer ties can be fostered through the working together process which is facilitated by the support given.

Getting support may also be very necessary when a certain project chosen can eventually unfold into being more than you are capable of handling. Therefore any added support that can be garnered will be very helpful indeed and you will not have to deal with the feelings of being overwhelmed.

Having the option of seeking support when needed also encourages those who lend the support to be able to bring a positive element into the otherwise slowly growing stressful situations. The support given, maybe physical or mental, both of which can help to foster positive elements. These elements maybe lacking at a particular juncture of the project, thus the support can fill this need.

How Procrastination Can Be A Downward Spiral

Procrastination can lead to a downward spiral. Here are some ways to avoid this destructive behavior pattern and also some recommendations to help overcome an already procrastinating mindset.

You Ought To Know

Starting a daily simple and non-demanding set of tasks list would allow you to venture into getting accustomed to a routine and being focused on completing the items on the list within the time frame allotted. In taking this first small step you are able to experience the satisfaction derived from the exercise of committing to completing tasks.

Without the practiced and sometimes forced ability to focus and start a task immediately, procrastination gains a foot hold into the situation. Thus by forcing yourself to begin and complete a task this negative element can be kept in check.

Sticking to tasks that can be immediately and easily done is one way to start you on actually achieving things on a daily basis. Learning to say "no" to a lot of things, and filtering only those that are immediately workable, will encourage the procrastinating nature to be abandoned.

Playing the waiting game is also another element that should be eliminated in the quest to avoid procrastination. Sometimes people develop the mind set of "ifs", this causes them to wait around until a particular condition or scenario is evident before they are willing to act. This form of procrastination will eventually lead to a lot of lost time and effort on the part of other who are more than willing to get the project started.

People who make it a habit of putting off things, end up never getting anything done. If left unchecked this habit can snowball and cause irreparable damage to you and those around. Vocalizing the intention of doing something and actually doing it are two very different scenarios, thus procrastination is indeed quite a destructive character trait. ***Get motivated.***

Energy Boosters

Without energy you will have a hard time motivating yourself for any length of time. Which affects you getting things done.

Motivation is the gasoline, energy is the engine!

Motivation and energy are intrinsically linked.

How do you increase your energy level? Here are some of the top ways:

1. **Stretching** – this releases tension from the muscles, helps to relax you and maintains good blood flow to the brain. You also make yourself more resistant to common muscle and joint injuries by keeping flexible.

2. **Exercise** – Ha, you knew this was coming ;-) A little gentle or moderate exercise over a sustained period of time will do wonders for your energy levels, not to mention your overall health.

3. **Cut Out The Caffeine** – sounds like the opposite of what you should do, but a caffeine high is then followed by a low. Switch to decaffeinated drinks and you will see an improvement in the consistency of your energy levels. Stay away from high caffeine *'energy'* drinks.

4. **Eat Regular Smaller Meals** – this helps keep your metabolism going, stops you snacking and makes sure your blood sugar stays consistent which is a big problem for most people. When you blood sugar drops then your energy will too.

5. **Take Some Time Off** – we all need a break every now and again. Getting away from our responsibilities for even a few hours can be a great way to recharge the batteries. Ditch the work, drop the kids off at friends and have a carefree night in with your partner.

6. **Breathe Deeply** – our bodies need oxygen, and if you slump your body compresses the chest and reduces the oxygen getting into your system. Get up, have a walk around when you feel lethargic and pull your shoulders back and get some good deep breaths down.

7. **Get Some Sleep** – Probably the most important, getting a decent night's sleep is a top priority. Take a half hour off before bed to read or do something leisurely to help your mind stop spinning through the day's problems. That way when you lie down you can actually try and get some sleep.

Motivation and keeping your energy levels up play a large part in being on your 'A' game and being productive. Be sure to recharge the energy levels often.

2: GETTING ORGANIZED

One of the secrets of being productive is to get your workspace and your personal life organized.

I've got to get my house office and personal life organized! When did you last speak these words? Was it when you recognized that you're literally drowning under gobs of paper? Perhaps it was when you got a look of the enormous laundry pile that you can never seem to catch up on. Maybe it was when you looked at all of the jumble in your kitchen, basement, bedroom, garage, den, front room and everywhere else. You might have even pondered tossing everything out the window! Was it when you urgently searched for those missing tickets? It may have been when you missed that crucial appointment. Or when that deadline sneaked up on you. Perhaps it was when you recognized that you had enough To Do's on your list to last you a lifespan. Was it when you urgently searched for that missing customer folder?

Or even worse, it might have occurred when you determined you had no time left for yourself, your kinsperson, your acquaintances, that needed holiday and basically everything in life that you love to do.

You're not alone. Those words have been expressed again and again by thousands of individuals all over the world. Disorganization may actually trap you into living a life filled with tension, frustration and bedlam. It may rob you of the precious time you ought to be spending enjoying your life. By defeating disorganization, you may be set free to live the sort of life you've always dreamed of. You deserve to be organized!

If you're sick of living in a maze of clutter or if you can't ever find what you need when you need it, you've come to the right place.

We'll help you to get your life organized, one-step at a time.

As a matter of fact, you may begin right now. What's the most disorganized area of your life—the one that makes you utterly crazy? Your closet? Your home office? The kids' game room? You may take the first step towards getting it organized today by producing a vision.

Get A Vision

1. Ascertain your goals.

Before you begin anything, ascertain its goal. If you don't know where you're going, how will you ever arrive there? Set mini-goals and reinforce yourself for successes.

Don't accept more than you may handle too soon, particularly if your goal is something outside your knowledge or present ability. It's easy to get disheartened when you recognize that your goal of running 3 miles a day has petered out after 2 weeks because you can't seem to get past one mile a day. Unless you've been an active runner it's better to begin slow and work your way up in increments. When you begin small and set mini-goals for yourself, you're much more likely to succeed.

You just began a job as a sales clerk and have a goal of becoming sales manager in 6 months. That's most likely not going to occur, and you're setting yourself up for letdown. Set goals that are getable by assessing the truth of the situation and gathering info. This is particularly crucial when setting goals where somebody else plays a pivotal role in whether you accomplish success, like your boss. It's great to aim big, but not so big that you can't accomplish your goal.

2. Unclutter your desk.

An uncluttered desk erases unneeded distractions and helps keep your mind on tasks that require immediate attention. Keep only the particulars on your desk that tie in to your current projects.

Clear the computer desk of paper. File most of the paperwork out of sight in clearly labeled folders. Place a cheat sheet on a nearby wall or under a keyboard for data that must be quickly accessed, like phone numbers and non-confidential account numbers; this will reduce the amount of paper on the desk. Limit pens and pencils on the desk surface to the few you use on a regular basis. Put most pens and pencils neatly away in a drawer. File DVDs, CDs and additional media storage items neatly into a notebook organizer for easy access.

3. Do not trust your memory.

You run the risk of letting undertakings fall through the cracks. The most beneficial way to never forget an appointment, a deadline or a particular again, is to write everything down.

An appointment book helps you to organize your time activities effectively. It enables you to prioritize activities according to their importance, when they have to be accomplished, and to plan ahead. For example, if you know the exact date of a crucial meeting a week beforehand, you are able to set aside time to prepare for it more effectively.

4. Consolidate like actions.

Rather than beginning and stopping at different levels of activity, you'll save time by doing all of your outgoing calls together, taking care of all your errands at one time, etc.

Consolidate the cooking by making triple batches and freezing. Make simpler meals nightly. Try to organize the grocery shopping so you only go once a week, once every 10 days, or even once every two weeks.

5. Clear out your files.

Before you go through the expense of buying more file cabinets, folders, etc., take the time to purge all unneeded paperwork and materials.

Separate the papers that are truly important like, bills, documents and receipts that you need to keep for tax purposes, statements etc.

6. Utilize one calendar.

The biggest error individuals make when utilizing planning calendars is to keep more than one. Keep personal, professional and family particulars on one calendar. It will help to wipe out scheduling conflicts. Remember, 'the man who wears two watches, never knows the right time.'

With today's hectic schedules, it frequently helps to run your email, calendar and reminders in one feature. Utilizing Microsoft Outlook's calendar feature will ensure that you'll never miss an engagement because you lost track of time surfing the Web.

7. Cut down phone tag.

Plan calls (whether to doctors, plumbers, clients, etc.) whenever possible. Have all essential materials in front of you. Write key questions down beforehand.

Register all your actions. Everything that needs to be remembered needs to be written someplace. Even when you've a privileged memory, nobody is perfect, it won't hurt anybody to write what you do in a paper just in case. Register phone numbers, appointments, birthdays, shopping lists, and to-do lists.

If you don't have time to organize a space from top to bottom, begin with the express version: remove only the clutter that's visible to the eye. The space will feel more organized, motivating you to tackle the rest of it in the near future.

Webster's defines clutter as *"a confused multitude of things"*. Look around the space you're decluttering and observe any items that are "confused" about where they belong—i.e., have no point being there—making any part of the space unusable. Instances are piles of schoolwork on the kitchen counter, shoes strewn about, stacks of old magazines, etc.

Easy Time Management

1. Arrange files for projects.

Don't waste time looking for papers when you need them. Keep all paperwork that pertains to a particular project together in one big folder. Among the most common ways to arrange files on your computer is according to date. Windows has many sorting functions to arrange your files such as by name, date, type and size. Sorting your files by date allows you to stay organized while having prompt access to your newest files.

2. Arrange time limits.

State, 'I've got only 5 minutes to talk.' Outline your phone calls, state, 'I'd like to discuss these 2 possible solutions to problem A . . .'

Make a schedule. Write it down on a piece of paper and stick with your schedule. While this might be the easiest step to do, it can be the hardest to follow.

3. Create time for yourself.

Make at least one screened appointment with yourself every day. Screened time is quiet, uninterrupted time allowing you to center on a project or catch up on your reading. Make lists and utilize them. You'll learn to be honest in how much you may accomplish in a given time.

4. Delegate.

Realize that you can't do everything. Delegate in the office and at home. To utilize an effective delegation system, you have to train, entrust, follow-up and evaluate. Brief the individual on the task: Define precisely what he is responsible for. Explain how the undertaking fits into the larger project. Clarify objectives and settle on deadlines.

5. Do not overfill file cabinets.

There's nothing worse than having to file papers in a filing cabinet that's overloaded! Leave adequate room in file drawers so you're not using all your energy to get a piece of paper in or out. Get busy doing away with any paper you don't need! Toss out info you no longer need, but doesn't require shredding. Recycle papers when you are able to. Try not to hang on to magazines and catalogs. These may really pile up.

6. Have fake deadlines.

If you've a deadline at the end of the month, record the deadline 4 days earlier. You'll eliminate the eleventh hour rush to complete the project as you'll have given yourself ample padding.

Take into consideration what might sidetrack you. The more time critical the task, the more crucial it is that you're realistic about what else is on your plate. Define each subtask, and set start and end dates for each. Make certain you continually evaluate how realistic your time frame is. If you're running out of time, then get creative and begin trimming tasks.

7. Utilize timekeepers and alarms.

Allocate time for your day-to-day activities, from working on projects to doing home chores. Then set timers or alarms to keep you on schedule. Set a PC alarm to draw your attention to an upcoming event or to wake you from a nap. Microsoft Outlook software has a reminder setting that may act as an alarm clock. It allows you to pick out the alarm sounds that will come through the computer speakers.

Remember that vision you created for the space you wish to organize? Most likely, it doesn't include the clutter living there! Your next step is to get rid of it. All of it.

Now comes the hard part—decision-making! A great organizing idea is to take four large bins or boxes and label them, "KEEP", "SELL", "DONATE" and "GARBAGE". The following step in getting organized is to now go through your stuff and place each item into one of these categories.

The beginning step in decluttering is mental. You have to make up your mind that you're ready to do it. It's like somebody going on a diet; telling an individual not to eat doesn't help. An individual will only lose weight when they make a decision to change the way they eat.

Decluttering is the same. The physical effort is less of a leap than the emotional/mental factor.

Time and Space

1. Make great utilization of space.

Add shelving for reference books and manuals. Add space extenders in desk drawers. Purchase full-suspension filing cabinets. Utilize stacking bins.

Pick out furniture with storage and space in mind. When buying a fold-out sofa, get one with a box underneath that's built to stow away linens. Purchase bunk beds for the kids that have a dresser attached to it. Pick taller, narrower dressers and bookshelves.

Rethink your options. An empty bottom drawer in your dresser may hold toiletries and beauty products you can't fit in the bath. Have a big suitcase that you seldom utilize? Store your bed sheets in it. Empty purses and carryalls may be used for stashing hats and socks. Bookshelves can likewise hold knickknacks.

2. Make the most of idle time.

People exhaust a lot of their time waiting. Waiting at a doctor's office, a bus stop or at an airport is commonplace. A lot of individuals may view waiting time as time lost, but waiting time doesn't have to be squandered time.

You are able to actually use this idle time to get some things done.

There are a lot of ways you are able to use waiting time more productively. Catch up on your reading while you wait for appointments. Audio cassettes of an educational or motivational nature are an excellent way to capitalize on your time while driving to work.

3. Get the youngsters off to their school day faster.

The trick is don't leave decision-making for the morning. The night prior, help your youngsters pick out their outfits, decide what they wish to eat and determine what they require for school. Pack lunches that night.

An assigned "sack lunch" bowl or basket is a great idea.

Beforehand, separate snacks into littler plastic bags that are easy to grab. Keep a loaf of bread and their favorite sandwich stuff like peanut butter and honey in there so when you make lunches all you have to do is snap up the basket and all the supplies are there.

This will likewise keep the lunch snacks and at home snacks separate so you won't be caught off guard when the supplies have to be replenished.

4. Set up quitting time.

If you have to work late, or during the weekend, set time limits for yourself. Whether you work for 2 or 4 hours, stop working at the end of that time and enjoy the rest of the evening or weekend.

Schedule your quitting time for each day - including weekends. My quitting time isn't truly a time of day, more along the lines of how many hours a day I'll put in. Every day is different.

5. What does it belong to?

Don't just toss your spare keys and other widgets in a shoebox without first identifying them. Label every item or packet. Labels are a crucial part of home organization. Making multi-use labels may reduce the time and effort you put into labeling things around your house. Although making labels that you are able to use over and over will require some effort, you'll save time and money by making the labels yourself.

6. Wipe out brushfires.

Brush fires are almost always caused by disorganization. Wipe out the disorganization and you'll eliminate the brush fires. Brushfires may consume a person's property. This is particularly true if a house or vehicle is swallowed up by a brushfire, which may demolish these items and leave burned-out hulks.

Even if personal property isn't completely consumed, the damage that brush fires may cause is frequently significant enough to require a great deal of repairs (rebuilding, repainting, etc.).

Brushfires may likewise destroy land, burning up grass and charring trees. A big brushfire can turn a beautiful parcel of land into a charred patch of dirt, making it worthless till everything grows.

7. Ascertain your most beneficial time for jobs.

Utilize your most productive time to do your most productive work. Awake in the morning? Afternoon?

Tackle your hardest, important work during the time of day when you're at your best and you're most likely to finish it.

If you spend ten minutes a day on your physical "inbox", it won't pile up. Attempt to touch each piece of paper once. And, don't open your mail without your calendar handy, a pad to make notes, your checkbook accessible, and a charge card memorized.

Bills may be put in the inbox to pay once a week. Invitations may be immediately put into your calendar and discarded (or if you're visual, posted on a message board till the date of the event), catalogs ought to be immediately discarded (and unsubscribe from them – there's nothing you can't get online that's in that catalog), and receipts may go into a small accordion file that separates them by month or subject).

Magazines ought to be placed where they're likely to be read (bedroom night table or briefcase to be read while commuting to work). Weekly issues are discarded weekly when the new edition arrives. Ditto for every day publications and every month publications.

Lists And Planning

1. Utilize control lists and to do lists.

Take charge of your time. When utilized properly, these effective tools give you a specific idea of what you have to accomplish. How many times have you've gotten someplace only to forget what you needed in the first place?

Note to self: Writing to-do lists saves time, energy, tension and even gas. A great list lets you forget--once you have a written reminder, your brain is free to center on other things. A to-do list even helps you meet your goals. Whether you're a legal pad, personal digital assistant (PDA) or back-of-the-phone-bill type, pick a scheme that works--and write it down!

2. Arrange firm deadlines.

Setting a deadline forces you to work toward it. Set a definite date and time. Stating, 'When I get a chance' or 'Sometime in the near future' is insufficient. Set your timeline for success. Be specific with the desired result.

Be realistic and kind to yourself. If you wish to see yourself succeed, do not create a situation only a super-hero may accomplish. Set your final goal, and work back, step-by-step to produce your timeline. Goals like learning a new skill, educational milestones, weight loss, and traveling, may all be attained within a timeframe.

Other goals, like spiritual growth and developing healthy habits, might continue throughout your life. With any type of goal, it helps to write down specifically what progressive steps you would like to achieve within a particular time frame.

3. Utilize a greeting card organizer.

Think about a greeting card organizer to remember birthdays, anniversaries and additional special events. These look like a notebook, except that every page has a monthly pocket to hold cards. You are able to pencil in birthdays, events, etc. for every month, plus, you are able to purchase your cards beforehand!

4. Design your garden ahead of time.

Begin planning your garden in the winter. Decide what you'll plant. Read up on the proper care of your plants, flowers and vegetables.

Sketch your garden out in writing. Grab a piece of paper and sketch out your ideas; your drawings don't have to be works of art as long as they help you envision your ideas. If you want something more detailed, plot your garden to scale on a piece of graph paper. When spring arrives you'll be prepared to 'grow.'

5. Stash away like items together.

Categorization is really crucial when you're getting organized. Keep all bill paying supplies in one place. Gather all of your craft provisions in a basket. Keep your photo supplies in one plastic bin. Utilize drawer dividers to keep any overflowing gadget or utensil drawers in check. After sectioning off drawers into smaller spaces, group similar items together for faster access.

6. Categorize your files.

First, decide on broad categories according to the specific work materials in your office. Then, file alphabetically or chronologically inside these categories.

Most individuals find that they end up having far too many categories and it becomes overwhelming. Labeling by month means you only have 12 to deal with. Second, many expenses don't neatly fit into one category. One single receipt from Target or Wal-Mart may fit under household goods, health-related purchases or tax-deductible business expenses.

7. Plan meals.

Plan your meals before you write out your grocery list. It will save time, as you'll know precisely what you need. Your meals ought to:

1) Be well-balanced and nutritious

2) Provide assortment

3) Be inside your food budget

4) Fit your time and energy limit

Plan what you will make with leftovers. For instance, if you're going to roast a chicken, the leftover chicken may be used to make a healthy chicken soup or salad.

If you wish to make hamburgers, purchase extra meat to use in chili or tacos. Choose 2 or 3 main dishes to make for the week. When combined with leftovers made into a different meal, you've healthy meals planned for the whole week.

All these tips that you read in this chapter are there to help you organize a certain area of your life. The more you can organize the easier it will be for you to become more productive and make being organized a habit.

3: PROCRASTINATING

Procrastination is a huge killer of being productive. It is therefore ideal that we discuss it in as much detail as possible in this immense chapter without dedicating the entire book to it.

Matters That Throw Us Off Our Course

Let's suppose you planned to be at your PC, working at a project, at 10 a.m. on a Monday morning, but you're not. How come? The answer may be one or more of the accompanying.

The Enemies:

➢ Woke up late.

➢ Scrapped with your lover last night, and continue reliving the quarrel in your brain.

➢ Are too sapped – the coffee hasn't set in yet.

➢ Are overly hyper – drank too much coffee and can't sit motionless.

➢ Are disquieted by the weather – it's amazing out and

you'd love to take a walk or bike ride.

➤ Are disquieted by the weather – it's atrocious and depressing.

➤ Got a telephone call (or e-mail or instant message) from a friend, who's depressed (though not in crisis) and asked to talk.

➤ Got a telephone call from a friend (or e-mail or instant message) that's happy and wished to share great news.

➤ Are reading the paper – every last word of it.

➤ Are surfing the internet or shopping online.

➤ Are playing Solitaire.

➤ Simply realized that it's highly crucial to work on another project.

➤ Or, if you work in a home office:

➤ Switched on the television set for "a minute" and saw that one of your favorite actors was being interviewed, so you decide to view the interview.

➤ Simply realized that the laundry urgently needs to get done!

➤ Facebook, Pinterest and other social media platforms.

These are common things that may throw you off your course. It's only a partial list; naturally, you may likely add many other entries to it. There are likely 100s of potential "bumps" that may knock you off your course.

One crucial thing to point out is that, while a few of these bumps appear "good" or "worthwhile" (like commiserating with your unhappy acquaintance or doing the laundry), and some seem "foul" or "frivolous" (like playing Solitaire), they're all equally unacceptable from the viewpoint of beating your procrastination habit.

You'll need to learn to resist the urge to get absorbed into activities not on your schedule, regardless how crucial or virtuous they appear at the moment. The one exception, naturally, is emergencies, by which I mean actions that can't be put off without significant harm to yourself or other people. However even with an emergency, after you've handled it, ask yourself whether it may have been prevented by finer planning, or whether somebody else could have handled it. If you've got a challenging goal, it's really crucial to learn to minimize the number of preventable emergencies in your life, and to learn to delegate as much as conceivable.

If it appears like I'm taking a hard line, I am. I have to, as procrastinators are frequently adept at rationalizing their diversions. Obviously, if somebody is ill or otherwise incapacitated, we ought to help them, but to what degree? It's not always clear, and a lot of procrastinators misjudge, sacrificing too much of their own time to assist other people, even when those other people aren't particularly needy or when somebody else is available to help. This issue may be hard to identify, much less solve, as the (deservedly) good feeling one gets from assisting frequently offsets the guilt that the procrastination commonly spawns.

View Your Commitments Differently

When you begin viewing your commitments from the viewpoint of somebody who's determined to succeed at their challenging dream – meaning, somebody who must utilize their time optimally, fresh solutions to formerly "unresolvable" quandaries frequently present themselves. So, for example:

➤ Your aged parents may likely find somebody else to mow their lawn and pick up the groceries like a different family member, or the high school youngster down the block who requires a few extra bucks. Or,

➤ Your mate and kids may likely survive on takeout (or cook their own food!) A couple of nights a week. Or,

> ➢ Your acquaintance who needs a lot of support may find other people or even professionals, like a therapist to help furnish it.

If you didn't have a challenging dream that you were following on top of life's average demands, then perhaps you could get away with mowing the lawn, fixing all the meals, and talking for hours daily with your friend.

However when you own up to your challenging dream, you're basically declaring that you'll be really particular and self-directed in how you spend your time, as you have to reserve as much time as possible for your aspiration. This is in direct contrast to most individuals, who let other people including family, friends, neighbors, colleagues and corporations control their time for them.

Nearly all ambitious dreamers, for example, have to reduce the time they spend on ho-hum household chores to as close as possible to zilch, so that they may utilize the reclaimed time and energy to work at their aspiration.

All right, if you like gardening and it feeds your soul, then don't quit. But washing? Yard work? Wiping up floors? Standing in line at the market? To the extent you're able to find somebody else to do it. Send your wash out to be done, hire somebody to maintain the lawn (or get your mate or children to do it), purchase a floor mopping robot, and have your foodstuffs delivered.

If you feel peculiar doing any of that, get over it: cutting down your housework burden is an investment in yourself. Likewise, it's unrealistic to believe that you may spend your time the same way non-ambitious dreamers do and yet achieve your challenging dream.

None of this ought to be taken to mean that you desert your loved ones or friends. It simply implies you invest your time judiciously. Even though you're not cutting your parents' lawn, for example, you may still be taking them to checkup appointments: that's a much higher value activity that's likely a far better utilization of your time.

And even though you're not fixing home cooked dinners nightly, you may still do it a few times a week. And even if you're not going to be able to speak to your friend for hours daily, you may still be available to her in times of true need.

It may be scary to alter the terms of our interaction with somebody, particularly if we've been interacting with them a particular way for years. (Double particularly if we've been taught to subordinate our needs to other people, as many women particularly are.)

Individuals frequently respond badly when we tell them we can't do as much for them, or spend as much time with them, as we have been. Frequently, however, if we take the time to share our state of affairs, aspirations and needs, they're surprisingly empathic and eager to help. So don't simply tell individuals you'll be less available tell them why, and invite their support and help.

If, after you share your story, a few individuals still aren't empathic, or are actively unfriendly, that's a sorry issue to have, but a typical one. That's why successful individuals learn to say "no", and also to distance themselves from unsupportive or toxic individuals, even if they happen to be related to them.

Whatever time you choose to spend helping other people you ought to build into your weekly or monthly schedule. You ought to likewise build in time both for your own relaxation and for unintentional events and emergencies.

Many individuals think time management is about attempting to stuff as much as possible into one's schedule, but it's not; it's regarding clearing as much as conceivable off your schedule so you may work, at a comfortable, non-stressful pace, on your crucial goals.

To summarize: whatever bumps you off your course that isn't an unpreventable emergency is procrastination, regardless how crucial it might seem at the time.

Desperation...and Promise

Many procrastinators tell themselves stuff like: "I'm lazy. I'm undisciplined. I'm a failure. I'm hopeless. I've got no self-control. I'll never win at anything."

Many creative persons, activists, and other ambitious dreamers take the self-abuse a step farther, framing their procrastination as a moral defect: "I'm a sellout, unattached, shallow".

A lot of procrastinators lead a double life, acting happy and productive while truly feeling hemmed in. Their boasts about their big workloads, power to work under pressure, and steady need to pull all-nighters are frequently just a cover for shame and despair; and frequently, when matters get really hot when they're about to miss a serious deadline, thereby showing their real, "shameful" nature they cut and run, deserting a project, class, job, relationship or other commitment."

Frequently, procrastinators become depressed almost as soon as they wake as they recognize they're destined to procrastinate that day. Procrastination may also feel really confusing.

At bedtime, you retrospect on the day and can't figure out where your time went. You remember reading the headlines, drinking a cup of java with your officemates, watching some TV, and surfing the net, but those random activities couldn't possibly have filled the whole day, could they? But, naturally, they did. Procrastination is, "the thief of time". To a procrastinator, it truly does feel as if his or her time were somehow stolen.

If a procrastination issue is severe enough, and lasts long enough, it's often called a "block", as in "writer's block". Anybody may be blocked, and many individuals, maybe most, are. Occasionally, blocks last for weeks or months, but oftentimes, tragically, they last for years, decades or even entire life spans. Being blocked is among the riskiest feelings in the world; it drives some individuals to absolute desperation.

But wait there's no need to feel ashamed or desperate! When

someone confesses to a procrastination issue, I congratulate her. Yes, congratulate. Here's how come: Procrastination is an affliction of ambitious individuals. If you don't trust me, do a net search on procrastination: you'll acquire links to 100s of pages advising you on how not to procrastinate while writing your novel or thesis, following a fitness program, or seeking a new career. These are all challenging endeavors, and individuals who follow them ought to be admired even if they do procrastinate.

All procrastinators, regardless how baffled, may boast at least one accomplishment: they haven't quit on their dream. If they had, they wouldn't be concerned about procrastinating on it.

To hang onto a challenging dream despite one's fears, and likewise (frequently) despite disheartenment and disapproval from those around us and society itself, requires vision, dedication and bravery. So, rather than seeing your procrastination issue as a shameful defect, attempt viewing it instead as a symbol of something enceinte inside you. Yeah, you've got a little work to do to recognize your full potential like who hasn't. But at least you continue showing up and fighting the great fight.

A different reason not to feel bad about your procrastination issue is that pretty much everybody procrastinates.

Let's likewise not forget that ambitious dreamers choose to follow exceptionally hard goals otherwise, they'd be ambitionless dreamers, right? Average life is pretty complex stuff, but in addition to the complexities of average life, ambitious dreamers may expect to face financial risk if not likely impoverishment; emotional risk and rejection; lack of support from loved ones and/or society; and nerve-wracking working conditions. And that doesn't even count the underlying difficulties of the goal itself i.e., the need of the person to perfect her craft and sell her work, or to finish a product.

A lot of individuals flee from these sorts of stresses, and I, for one, can't blame them. The issue, however, is that in doing so they likewise flee from their aspirations. Whenever I teach, I remind my pupils who are frequently deeply ashamed of their procrastination issue of the many individuals who have given up on their aspirations.

We all share a minute of sadness for those individuals, and then I softly congratulate my pupils for persevering in their own aspirations despite all the difficulties and barriers.

Recognizing The Issue

Look, you're a smart individual. A creative individual. A dedicated individual. I'm pretty certain about all of that, or you wouldn't be an ambitious dreamer, or reading this e-book. So, how come you can't resolve a little procrastination issue?

If you're like a lot of people, that question has haunted you for a long time. Among the most frustrating things about procrastination is that it appears like it would be the simplest issue in the world to resolve. Actually, it's among the hardest. Really, that's not quite true. Any issue is difficult to solve, if you're not truly solving it.

I mean it: the only way to resolve an issue is to resolve it. If you attempt to resolve an issue utilizing actions designed to resolve some other issue, or actions designed to resolve no issue at all, but rather to maintain the status quo, then you're bound to bomb. You may try from here to the moon, reining in all the mental capacity, creativity and passion you may muster, and you'll still never resolve the issue.

The Problem

You likely believe the root issue causing your procrastination is laziness, lack of discipline, lack of self-control, immaturity, lack of commitment, or some similar character defect. But guess what? It's probably none of those.

Firstly, most procrastinators are not I repeat, not lazy, undisciplined, etc. As a matter of fact, most tend to be dynamos in areas other than the one they're procrastinating in. Among the peculiar agonies of procrastination is that we're frequently productive in areas of our lives other than the one closest to our heart.

Secondly applying damaging labels like "lazy" or "undisciplined" to yourself is, from a problem-solving standpoint, worse than worthless. Not only do those labels misidentify the issue, they really make the situation worse by sabotaging your self-assurance and predisposing you to failure.

Moreover, people frequently live up or down to the labels; so that if somebody repeatedly calls you, or you repeatedly call yourself, lazy or uncommitted, you're likely to live "down" to that label.

More often than not, solving, or resolving, an issue is a rather trivial exercise when we understand what the problem is. Treating procrastination as a symptom of laziness or a lack of discipline doesn't work, as those are not the causes of procrastination. Instead, they're symptoms, just like procrastination itself is a symptom, of a deeper issue. That issue is commonly either:

You were never taught the habits of productive work. As we live in a vacuum, this likely means you've rather learned the "default" habits of low productivity or non-productivity.

This results in what I call Behavior Based Procrastination.

Or,

Fear: of change, success, failure, etc.

This results in what I call Dread Based Procrastination.

Frequently, individuals suffer from both.

Behavior Based Procrastination is a comparatively easy issue to define and solve.

Dread Based Procrastination is more complex. Unlike Behavior Based Procrastination, which is commonly caused by a lack of data or training, dread Based Procrastination is caused by, as its name implies, concern.

Dread is unfortunately a major force in a lot of people's lives: it's frequently a rational, if not optimal, reaction to the troubles and stresses of life and an ambitious path.

Success Obstacles

Dread Based Procrastination's disguises itself by mimicking productivity. It does this, commonly, by generating one of four characteristic anti-productive behaviors: perfectionism, negativity, hypersensitivity and panic. Most procrastinators are prone to at least one of them, and most are prone to all 4.

Panic deserves a special mention. It's not truly an obstacle in and of itself, but acts as an obstacle "amplifier", blowing your fears out of symmetry and increasing the odds that you'll move back into one of the anti-productive behaviors. The job of defeating dread based procrastination is basically the job of overcoming panic, so that when you experience an instance of dread, doubt or discomfort, you don't become overwhelmed by it and get bumped off your course."

What Holds You Back

There are likewise 2 other categories of obstacles that are not in themselves dread based, but that are frequently present:

The first are Logistic Obstacles, which are commonly caused by simple ignorance. For instance:

➢ Deficiency of a clearly outlined mission and/or path to success

➢ Deficiency of time management

➢ Deficiency of planning, skills, resources and/or facilities

➢ Deficiency of mentors or other support

Put differently, you either don't know what you're supposed to be doing, or lack the skills or resources to do it. A typical individual suffering from a logistic obstacle would be a business owner who doesn't recognize she ought to be spending at least half her time promoting and selling, and thus spends her time on more insignificant jobs.

Basic resolutions to logistic obstacles include: doing mission management and time management, organizing your office, purchasing some new equipment, taking a course, and setting up regular consultations with mentors.

When you commit to overcoming a logistic obstacle, it's frequently not hard to do so. If you do have trouble overcoming yours if you appear to lack the "self-control" to make the resolution work, or can't even find the time to consider the issue then you likely also suffer from dread based procrastination. You'll likely have to deal with the dread first, before you may move on to the more superficial logistical fix.

There are likewise what I call Situation Obstacles, which involve others or additional conditions outside your full control. A hard day job, heavy family responsibilities, and an unsupportive mate are situation obstacles. So are a disability and serious ill health.

Situation obstacles are frequently the hardest to overcome. Their resolutions frequently involve major life changes like changing jobs, leaving relationships, changing life-styles, compromising on one's treasured goals, or committing to person or couple's therapy.

Like logistic obstacles, situation obstacles commonly occur alongside dread based procrastination, and so you'll first have to deal at least partly with your dreads before you may effectively begin changing your situation. But even once you work past the dread, you're still left having to deal with some really hard circumstances.

The most crucial thing you have to know about your obstacles is that all of them may be overpowered. It doesn't matter who you are, how you were raised, what race, religion, nationality or sex you are, or how much cash you have. All of your obstacles may be overpowered.

Overpowering an obstacle might not be simple. It might not be fun. It could take months, years or even decades. It might take time and cash. But it may be accomplished. By "overcome," I mean annihilated, minimized or compensated for.

You might have a disability that you have to live with, or have experienced an awful loss from which the hurt will never entirely disappear. But you may still work to at least minimize the damaging effect of your ill luck on your future success.

Did I state that all of your obstacles may be overpowered? What I truly meant to state is that all of your obstacles have to be overpowered. As what other choice, truly, do you have? Failure to overcome your obstacles leads to a life of bitterness and diminished potential.

The procedure of overcoming your obstacles is the really essence of the human journey. If you've been procrastinating a while, you're likely demoralized and have lost sight of your strengths, gifts and virtues.

Once you quit running from your obstacles and begin working to overpower them, you'll reclaim those favorable qualities and likewise probably discover a few wonderful new ones. This procedure of reclamation and growth is among life's most amazing and joyful experiences.

3 Productivity Actions

All productive work may be broken down into these 3 actions:

1. Arriving to work exactly when you're supposed to.

2. Directly beginning the work you're supposed to be doing.

3. Remaining centered on the work for 20 minutes or more.

These actions are the essence of productive work. They're likewise the points at which procrastination occurs, and, consequently, the points at which it may be attacked.

A Plan

In action #1, the word "exactly" means precisely. 8:00 a.m., not 8:01, 8:05, or even 8:00:10. You have to train yourself to be precisely where you're supposed to be not thinking of it, not on the way, not pouring a cup of coffee at the precise moment you're supposed to be there.

In action #2, the word "directly" means that, about a minute after your butt hits the chair, you start your work. "The work you're supposed to be doing" ought to be self-explanatory by now, but let's be extra heedful and remind ourselves that ad lib unscheduled calls (even "urgent" ones), coffee sipping, paper reading, net surfing, and additional activities are all procrastination, pure and simple.

So is doing other work even crucial, good feeling work that wasn't scheduled for this period. You may spend your complete life immersed in these activities, and make little or no progress on your most crucial goals.

In action #3, the word "centered" means that you're flirting with your task, and only your task. Put differently, you're not thinking of other work you may be doing, or your worries regarding your task, or philosophical issues related to your task. And, naturally, you're not thinking of your personal life, last night's TV program, or the birds cheeping enticingly outside your window.

"20 minutes or more." The amount of time one may, or should, remain centered on work differs from person to person. Most individuals, however, may train themselves to work in a centered manner for at least 20 minutes before having to get up and take a break.

After your break and your breaks ought to be as long as you need them to be, particularly when you're 1st tackling your procrastination issue you may return to work for another 20 minutes.

At first, however, working for 20 minutes might seem as unrealistic as flying to the moon. So begin with 10 minutes, or 5, or 2 if you have to. Then, take as long a break as you require, praise yourself for your accomplishment, and repeat.

As you become more and more comfortable with your work, you may build up to 10 minutes of sustained work, then 15, 20, 30, etc. The key is to be patient and not push it.

Using Productivity Actions

Now that you comprehend the 3 productivity actions more fully, you may start practicing them. There are 5 keys to success:

1. Begin little, and aspire for tiny advances

2. Extravagantly reinforce each tiny success

3. Dismiss "failures" except to acquire knowledge out of them

4. Expect plateaus and lapsing

5. Stay at it!

Utilize It

1. Begin little and aspire for tiny advances

"Begin little" stands for practicing the 3 productivity actions (a.k.a., "not procrastinating") on no more than 2 or 3 tasks at a time and the tasks you practice on ought to be simple ones. Beginning with that novel you've been blocked on for 10 years is likely an unsound idea.

Household chores are an excellent thing to at the start practice on as we tend to procrastinate on them not out of dread, but merely because they're ho-hum. So practice not procrastinating on washing up the dishes or laundry (or mowing the lawn, or taking the automobile in for an oil change, and so forth.), if those are jobs you routinely procrastinate on. (Practice actions #1 and #2 only, obviously you don't wish to spend a lot of time doing chores.) Easy personal care tasks like flossing and taking vitamins are additional great candidates for practice.

If the tasks you're practicing on appear embarrassingly little or trivial, you're doing it precisely right! The key is to get used to the feeling of not procrastinating, and you'll only have the chance to do so if you at first practice on activities that offer a high chance of success. Likewise, pay attention to the (likely numerous) areas of your life where you don't procrastinate, and observe the feeling of sedate self-command you have while approaching those tasks.

It's that same feeling you're aiming to arouse around the tasks you're presently procrastinating on and are well on your way to resolving the issue. (Yes, you're aiming to produce particular feelings inside yourself. successful individuals consciously work to accomplish particular moods, as opposed to passively accepting whatever emotions happen to grab them. A lot of unsuccessful individuals, in contrast, don't even recognize that that's even possible to accomplish.)

Go on practicing the 3 productivity actions on easy stuff, and you'll by nature get better at not procrastinating. You'll then go less afraid, ambivalent and conflicted, and begin to make the essential shift from viewing procrastination as an inherent character defect to seeing it as a behavioral issue you may resolve. In the meantime, getting the dishes done, flossing regularly, and so forth, will themselves have a beneficent outcome on your mood, and likewise empower you to arrive at more changes.

Only after you've gotten good at not procrastinating on the trivial junk should you start practicing it on your other ambitious endeavor. Now, it's doubly crucial for you to begin small. If you're a writer, don't set out to put down an entire chapter, but only a page or paragraph. Or, if you're an entrepreneur, don't aim to spend the whole morning doing sales calls, but only 10 minutes.

Put differently, when operating in the scary realm, begin very small. And merely after you've gotten great at not procrastinating at tiny tasks, do you take on the greater ones. And only after you've gotten great at doing the actions for 10 minutes (or 5, or 2, or whatever works for you at first), do you begin practicing action #3 slowly working up your endurance so that you may do your scary work for 15, 20, 30, etc., minutes at a time.

If you abide by my advice to "begin little", you'll have many successes, by which I mean cases when you were able to reject procrastinating and get right to work. It's crucial, in those cases, to celebrate your accomplishment! Pat yourself on the back, indulge in a treat, and broadly make a fuss over yourself. This sort of positive reinforcement not only advances your confidence and betters your mood, but helps imprint your accomplishment in your memory so that you may call on it when required. It doesn't matter how little the accomplishment is. Even if it's something as easy as taking your vitamins precisely when planned or taking them at all, if you often neglect to give yourself at least a mental pat on the back. For greater accomplishments, make certain to make a huge fuss and give yourself some sort of tangible reward.

When a youngster fails to meet a goal, the mean parent tends to criticize and blame, while the good, effective parent provides compassion and understanding. The good parent likewise helps the youngster keep the failure in perspective, reminding him that the "failure" likely isn't as dreadful as he thinks it is, and that there are plenty of other things he has succeeded at. With the good parent's help, the youngster grows up to be a resilient grownup that is not so afraid of failure that he procrastinates.

You have to be your own good parent, which means that whenever you bomb at not procrastinating or another goal, you shouldn't criticize or blame yourself, but rather respond with compassionate objectivity. Critique, depletes your self-regard, sabotages your self-assurance, mischaracterizes the issue, and only makes things worse. Rather, be a compassionate observer and analyst of your situation, holding in mind that there are frequently perfectly great reasons behind procrastination, even if the procrastination reaction itself isn't optimal. The proper reaction to failure is to ponder it just long enough to come up with a resolution so that the same thing doesn't occur again:

A plateau is when you stay stuck at a level of accomplishment in spite of repeated attempts to move ahead. Lapsing is when you really lose ground and get less effective. Both are discouraging, and yet both are an inevitable piece of any personal growth process. If you've an "off" day, week, month or year, don't pick apart, or shame or blame yourself: simply accept it for what it is, and hope to do better shortly.

Plateaus and lapsing frequently indicate that you're setting too ambitious goals. If that's indeed the case, the resolution is to go back to a prior level of achievement you're comfortable with and remain there for a while till you find your confidence. Then, remember to set humbler and attainable goals in the future.

Plateaus and lapsing may likewise indicate that you're experiencing personal or other issues that are interfering with your ability to do your work. Most of us may tackle only one major issue at a time and, let's face it, a lot of issues, including sickness or a financial crisis, may take precedence even over making progress on our earnest dream. If something does pull you away from your aspiration, just do what you have to do without shame or remorse or regret. Finally, you'll be able to return to your work quite possibly bringing to it a richer perspective as a result of your "sabbatical".

Those who succeed are forever those who hang in. Occasionally, they have to temporarily put their challenging dream aside while they work at other priorities. But they forever come back to it. They never quit and neither should you.

5 Success Hints

Tips to get you moving down the road to beat procrastination.

Follow This

> ➢ Forever Start Your Day with a Schedule

Scheduling is crucial as vagueness opens the door to the sorts of fears and doubts that may lead to procrastination.

Ideally, you'll know how to produce a manageable schedule that reflects your core values. If not, at least come up with a easy schedule that states specifically what you're going to be doing or working on each hour of the day. Attempt to produce your schedule the night before so that the act of scheduling itself doesn't itself become a sort of procrastination.

> ➤ Be Prepared

The Boy Scouts got this one right. For the same reason as #1, above to prevent confusion that may throw you off your course you have to start your day with all the data, tools, and materials required to achieve your work right out there in front of you.

That signifies everything: books, paper files, PC files, phone numbers, writing implements, even paper clips. It ought to all be available, organized and in perfect working order. (Cellular phone charged? Pencils sharpened?)

Note: If, despite repeated tries, you're unable to show up for work scheduled and prepared, that might be a sign that you've a high level of dread that's causing you to procrastinate.

> ➤ Approach Your Work Without Hesitation

Remember how productivity action #1 is showing up to work on time, and productivity action #2 is getting right to work on the right stuff? While practicing those actions, attempt not to hesitate. Hesitation gives your thoughts time to wander, and if you've got a procrastination habit, they'll frequently wander directly towards your dreads. (Now you comprehend the meaning of the proverb "he who hesitates is lost.")

Rehearse gliding over to your desk and beginning your work with no hesitation.

> ➤ Remain Calm

Strong emotions, ricochet you off your course. They likewise make it harder for you to stay centered on the present so that you are able to practice the 3 productivity actions. Work, therefore, to stay calm as the clock ticks towards your start time. If you catch yourself feeling dread, anxiety or uncertainty, gently reassure yourself. (E.g., "I'm just going to write for 10 minutes – that's all. Then I may take a break.")

If necessary, put yourself in a little "trance" simply long enough for you to glide over to your desk and begin working, as our dreads are frequently strongest before we actually begin our work and disappear if we just persist for a couple of minutes.

> ➤ Don't Make Your Work Harder Than It Is

Don't fall into the trap of presuming that procrastination is inevitable. Popular culture likes to portray the act of production as a sort of epic battle because it makes great drama, but that's the inappropriate model to follow. Rather, you ought to approach your work with a light touch, and the experience ought to be like play: simple, safe and fun.

If your project appears scarily huge or crucial, attempt breaking it down into small no, tiny chunks and working on those one at a time, while brushing off, for the time being, the big picture. This sounds like petty advice, but it's essential, and many successful ambitious dreamers have learned to do this mechanically. (And don't forget to have fun!)

Frequently, all the same, when our work isn't fun, it's because we're fearful or panicked, either about the work itself or something else in our life. As you now know, attempting to work past that dread is frequently futile, particularly if the effort is accompanied by self-criticism. Our only true course is to bravely face down and explore our dreads, and the conditions surrounding them.

Even in moments of non-motivation, act as if you're extremely motivated. This is because of a fantastic thing that behavioral scientists have discovered: that not only do our emotions order our actions, but our actions often order our emotions.

Research has demonstrated, for example, that we don't simply smile because we're pleased, we in reality get happier when we smile. That's because the smile originates a sequence of hormonal and additional events that relaxes us and makes us feel great.

Professional sales people, who have to be "on" close to a hundred percent of the time in order to make their quotas, are really familiar with this phenomenon: they're taught that their posture, expression and other physical attributes impact not only their mood but their customers'.

They're taught to grin even when talking over the phone, as although the client on the other end of the line can't see them do it, the salesperson's voice sounds much more forceful and dynamic when she grins. Try it.

A lot of sales people, performers, athletes and other peak performers formulate a personal collection of tricks, rituals, and physical and mental exercises to help themselves get and stay pumped for their workday. You ought to do the same thing.

And here's the frosting on the cake, the astonishing secret that empowered individuals in every field eventually learn: that with enough practice mimicking peak performance; you'll actually begin experiencing the real thing more frequently.

Experts say that while we can't operate at peak all the time, we may likely do so much more frequently than we recognize. Merely by practicing at performing at peak, you are able to train yourself to enter into peak much more easily and often.

And that will be the most astonishing reward of all, for all of your hard work.

4: THE ULTIMATE RESULT™ METHOD

In order to help my business clients and my coaching clients to become more productive, more successful, more valuable, I have created the Ultimate RESULT™ Method.

The Ultimate RESULT™ Method is an outline of the method that you can use to start creating a way to become more productive in your daily tasks.

The RESULT™ stands for:

R - Require: The fundamental requirement to being able to improve your productivity is to know what you need to accomplish and to know how to accomplish your tasks.

E - Evaluate: You need to evaluate which tasks take priority.

S - Systems: You need to create systems to help you handle your routine tasks efficiently.

U - Update: You need to keep your systems updated as you progress and keep on refining them to help improve productivity.

L - Limit: You need to limit distractions as much as possible as these are the productivity killers.

T - Tools: You need to know which tools work best for you and you need to know how to use them effectively.

Everything in this book forms some part of the Ultimate RESULT™ Method.

You can have all the tools in the world and know how to use them, however if you cannot put them together to work in synergy with each other, then they are no more useful at increasing your productivity than using them on their own.

Let's take a look at the 10 Steps to productivity, put together by Michael Sliwinski, which comes from David Allen's *"Getting Things Done"*. Michael has reviewed all the best and greatest systems out there and this one stands out from the crowd. You can find out more about Michael at http://www.nozbe.com

This is the productivity system that I use and that my clients see results with.

Michael has a great tool called Nozbe and he uses it in his 10 Steps to Ultimate Productivity system. You don't need to use Nozbe if you don't want to. Simply substitute any applicable tool that does a similar task for you.

Here is the breakdown of the steps that we will be looking at in greater detail later on in this chapter as explained by Michael:

Step 1 in the course is about "Clearing your mind" and putting everything into your trusted system. We'll talk about Inboxes and how to use them, to make sure your mind is focused and nothing gets forgotten.

Step 2 is about organizing your tasks into projects. About dividing the big tasks into small, actionable steps to ensure you'll always get them done. You'll become a project management ninja after this lesson.

Step 3 is about defining your "next actions" - your priority tasks that need to be done next to keep your projects moving forward.

You'll learn that sometimes it takes getting just one small task done to move an avalanche of a project forward and begin accomplishing your goals.

Step 4 is about being productive anywhere. Using your computer, smartphone or tablet. Today's era of technology enables us to get tasks done anywhere and have more free time later!

Step 5 is about collaborating. We live in a connected world and your colleagues as well as your close friends can help you get a lot more done. You'll learn how to share projects, delegate tasks and communicate through them effectively.

Step 6 is about working in contexts - it's a second, and very helpful layer of productivity, where you divide tasks not only into projects, but into places these can be done in, tools these can be done with, and so on.

Step 7 is about managing your reference material and documents. Store your notes and digitize as much content as you can to make sure to have it at hand when you're getting your tasks done. Lots of tricks and apps can help you with that.

Step 8 is about reviewing your recently set up productivity system. At least once a week you need to have a meeting with yourself and review your tasks, projects, lists and goals. Learn to start your next week fresh!

Step 9 is about Email and how to handle it. How to process it to zero and how to handle others' expectations when it comes to an email reply. How to make sure you don't get lost in the flood of email messages coming in.

Step 10 is where I help you start with everything you've learned so far. I will add several tips and tricks that work for me and point you toward additional materials for inspiration for action.

Now that we know what the 10 steps are about it is time to get intimate with them. Here they are as written by Michael himself.

Step 1

Welcome to Step 1 of our 10 steps. Here we'll deal with the fact that you are thinking about too many things at once. You need to take stuff off your mind and put it all in your trusted productivity system.

My wife always laughs at me saying I'm like an old computer with default settings - I recognize only 16 basic colors and I pretend to be a multi-tasking guy... where, actually, I can only do one thing at a time.

I must admit there is some truth in that. Just like David Allen says in his book "Getting Things Done", when your mind has too much to think about, you can't actually get anything done. You can't work efficiently when your mind is being distracted.

That's why you need your trusted system where you can easily put stuff into it. The easier you can throw stuff at it, the better. That's the first secret. The second is to make sure you process this stuff later.

The place you put stuff into is called an "Inbox" - a place where all of your thoughts, files, documents, notes, emails, voicemails... where all of your inputs go.

The problem is, we've got more than one "inbox" in our lives. Actually, a lot more than one. The solution is to narrow them down to as few as possible and be aware of all of them. And process these inboxes on a regular basis.

Processing is key. You don't "take a look at your inbox" or "glance" at it. You process an inbox by going through each and every item in the inbox and deciding what to do with it.

Some inboxes are physical, some are virtual. Or "in the cloud" as we say it. But they are all there. Here's the list of my inboxes and how I deal with them... and I have a few!

Email Inbox - all of the emails I'm receiving. I go through each and every email message to make sure my Email inbox stays at ZERO every day. I don't respond to each message, I move some of them to a "respond later" folder. The key is to decide what to do with each email.

Physical Inbox - a place in my office where I automatically put all the stuff that comes to me like documents, letters, receipts... - I process it at least once a week to ZERO. Again, I decide on each item if I should toss it, destroy it, keep it, scan it... and move on to the next one.

A trick I use often is to have a "paper pad" handy on my desk. When a thought comes in, I just write it down there. By the end of the day I have it full with many random notes. I just put the piece of paper in my physical inbox and process it later.

Nozbe Inbox - the inbox in my task manager of choice - I put all of the tasks that come to my mind there. At least once a week I need to clean up this mess and decide what to do with each task - if it's something I want to add to my current list of active projects, or if it's something I'll do someday... maybe...

It's important that my "virtual" inbox in Nozbe is as flexible as my physical inbox. I can forward an email to Nozbe with a task name written in the subject line. I can also add a task from any browser with a bookmarklet or simply add a task to my desktop version of Nozbe with a global keyboard shortcut.

I use a popular app called Evernote to store my notes and access them from anywhere. Evernote syncs with Nozbe and it helps me process my tasks even more. When I tag a note with an "Inbox" tag or with a name of an active project, I make it viewable from within Nozbe.

When I didn't have the time to type, I'd just pull out my iPhone and click on "Voice Memos" app and dictate something I had on my mind. I'd process these voice memos every week. Now that Nozbe accepts voice-dictated tasks on my iPhone, I dictate tasks directly there.

I also use apps like "Pocket" or "Instapaper". Here, I put all of the interesting articles I found somewhere on the Internet. This way when I feel like reading - I open this app on my iPhone or iPad and just read. This way I have a batch of fresh content to absorb every single day.

On my Mac I have a "Downloads" folder - it's the default folder in my browsers that holds all downloaded files, apps or documents... they all go there. Again, every week I make sure to process this folder and clean it up and decide what to do with each and every downloaded file.

I have several inboxes: physical Inbox, Nozbe inbox, Evernote, Voice memos, Read-it-later app and the Downloads folder. It's important that I don't put incoming stuff anywhere else.

The next key thing is that I know when I process these inboxes. Some are being processed every day, some every other day, all of them at least once a week. Again, if one week I don't clear something out, it's going to haunt me over the course of the next days. These inboxes need to be cleared out every week.

This is the first part of 10 steps - the Inbox - why and where we should put our thoughts to ensure that we don't lose them and most of all, to keep our head clean and clear of distractions. This way we can keep our mind focused on the tasks at hand.

Step 2

Step 2 is about organizing your tasks into projects. About dividing the big tasks into small, actionable steps to ensure you'll always get them done. You'll become a project management ninja after this lesson.

Here I'll show you that what you used to think as a task, might actually be a project... when it requires more tasks to complete. You'll learn to create many more projects for yourself than you used to.

Like it or not, you will become a Project Manager. We tend to think Project Managers are the guys who manage big investments, take-overs or big deals. We are all Project Managers as we manage our day-to-day tasks and projects of our lives.

Anything that requires more than one thing to do is a project. Here's a list of possible projects: - "Birthday for my brother" - all the tasks that require organizing a birthday party - "Presentation for a meeting" - things to prepare like: outline, sketch, slides, clipart, and more. I guess you get the idea.

It's easy to fall into the trap of adding a project as one task... and the task in our eyes becomes huge and unmanageable. That's why if something requires more steps, make it a project and divide it into small, manageable tasks.

This happens to me all the time. Very often I convert a task to a project when I see it becoming bigger and more important and requiring at least two or three steps. I often start with a task and later "escalate it" to a project.

I keep the names of my projects short, yet try to make them as descriptive as possible. When I started creating Nozbe it was also my only project on my list. With the amount of different type of activities my application has created, I had to split this project into "Nozbe development", "Nozbe marketing", and many more...

The thing is, I'd rather have more projects than less. Contrary to what you might think, more projects means more transparency. With more projects I see all of my pending activities at one glance. Following the example with the "Nozbe" projects I have more than 20 projects associated with Nozbe these days.

With today's technology and apps like Nozbe, I can move tasks, notes and files between projects easily (with few clicks) and I do it very often. Nothing is set in stone, as the tasks get done, many projects change and morph... and tasks migrate.

I prefer co-projects to sub-projects. Hierarchy can be very limiting. I prefer to have similar projects on the side rather than sub-projects. This is why in Nozbe we have project labels that group projects together.

Some of my projects have several labels, others have only one. My "Blog" project can be filed under "Nozbe" label if it's a Nozbe's blog as well as a "Writing" label that groups all my writing activities.

Labeling projects helps me maintain focus - something we talked about in Step 1. With labels I can filter the list of projects I want to see at each point in time. Even though I have around 50 active projects, I can see only 5-10 of them at a time, depending on the label.

I love to keep things simple. Adding priorities to projects or tasks feels like over-complicating the picture. I prefer just to re-organize projects with drag-and-drop in Nozbe. Projects on the top of the list have higher priorities. That's it.

And if I have trouble finding a particular project or prefer to have an "ordered list" I can switch to the "alphabetical order" of the project list. Many productivity gurus suggest to keep your project list alphabetical.

Some projects have a clear "completion time" - meaning, they will be "done" at some point in time. Once all the tasks are "done" in these projects I'll just mark them as "complete" and have them gone from my list.

However, I also treat projects as "lists", meaning that some projects like "blogging ideas", "being superdad", "Nozbe marketing" are never going to end as these projects keep on receiving tasks all of the time. And that's OK, too.

Projects are not only tasks. Projects need reference or research material. In Nozbe we use notes and files as for that. These are very important when you're doing a research for your project.

We also like other great apps like Dropbox and Evernote. That's why we have a built-in syncing mechanism with these apps. Files and notes in these apps appear to relevant projects in Nozbe automagically as reference material.

To empower you to get your tasks in projects done, you can

attach to tasks all of the reference materials you collected. You can simply comment on a task with a file, image, Youtube video, Evernote note, Dropbox file, whatever you want.

So there you are - a project manager. That's right - it's a reality that all of us busy professionals must embrace. Being productive means cranking those tasks first and later getting the projects done.

Are your tasks big and scary? Break them down into projects, slice them to pieces and get them done one by one. Collect your relevant reference material and when you learn these habits well, you'll become a master Project manager.

Step 3

Step 3 is about defining your "next actions" - your priority tasks that need to be done next to keep your projects moving forward. You'll learn that sometimes it takes getting just one small task done to move an avalanche of a project forward and begin accomplishing your goals.

Here I'll try to help you find that next physical task that helps you get closer to getting a project done. You'll ask yourself many times over: "What's my next action here?"

To me, the "Next Actions" concept is the killer feature of the Getting Things Done system by David Allen. The concept of having so many tasks and deciding on the "next physical action that moves things forward" proved to be a very powerful technique for me.

When I discovered the book by David Allen and read it, I understood what's the difference between traditional to-do lists and tasks managers ... and applications based on or inspired by Getting Things Done... like Nozbe :-)

The problem: If you did what I asked you to do in the previous two steps, you ended up with long, overwhelming to-do lists in many, many projects I just asked you to create. Lots of projects, lots of tasks, where to start?

There is a solution: Any time you have created a new project, please carefully look at your list of tasks for this project and ask yourself – what's the next action? Which task should I do now to feel I'm moving this project forward towards its completion?

Why is it so powerful? Because you're no longer looking at a list as a waterfall... meaning that you would need to start with the first task, then the second, then the third... and so on. Sometimes the first task is the one that's blocking you and you're not moving the project forward!

The key lies in the theory of "small victories" meaning if you can do something, anything in the project, you'll feel better, you'll see that you're moving forward and the project is not standing still. You are getting things done.

Sometimes it's about choosing a task that's easy, from the middle of the list of your tasks, just to feel better. Like you have to call 10 people to invite them to a meeting, start with calling the ones you like most first.

In Nozbe the "Next Action" concept is at the core of the application. To create a "next action" all you have to do is mark a task with a star... That's it. You literally "star" a task. And then it shows up on your "starred" task list which we call "Priority" list.

You can "star" a few tasks in one project if you want to. I choose between 0 and 3, meaning some projects don't have any next actions (at least for now), others have one, or maybe two, or three. The idea is to have the Priority list as short as possible to process it fast and have a warm and fuzzy feeling of being in control.

We borrowed the concept of "star" from Google Mail where you can "star" an email. The idea is that when you have starred the tasks in your projects, you are later able to see a list of all of these tasks from all of these projects on one Priority list.

This way you don't have to review all of your projects every day to search for "next actions" – you have your current list of next actions at hand, and you need to focus on getting these done. Once the list is empty, go search for new "starred" tasks.

Again, when you're getting your "starred" task list done, don't think too much about "prioritizing" beyond what's necessary – just focus on the next task at hand and if you feel like doing another task from the list, move it upwards and get it done.

As you can tell, I'm not a big fan of prioritizing – Nozbe was designed to be a "task doer" and not a "task manager" – you don't want to spend time managing tasks, you want to get them done. Focus on that. That's why reordering with drag and drop is so easy in Nozbe.

The order of your tasks on your Priority list is independent of the order of these tasks in their projects. Furthermore, to make sure your Priority list feels like your command center, in Nozbe some of the tasks get "starred" automatically.

Like when a task has a due date of "today", it's automatically starred and shows up on your Priority task list. Without you having to think about it. This way you won't miss any due date or appointment.

When you are sharing a project with your team and a task is being delegated to you – you become responsible for the task and it's being starred for you. Again, this way you won't lose track of it either.

Your Priority task list in Nozbe can be filtered by project, context, time and other things so you can narrow it down to even less tasks and focus on the ones on your screen. More focus, more tasks get done.

It's important to remember – don't mark all of your tasks as "next actions" – this would defeat the purpose. It's really OK when some of your projects have 0 next actions at this moment, because you choose not to move them forward right now, and it's OK this way.

In a nutshell – first review your projects, second, in some of them mark a task with a star and later get all of these "starred" tasks done in your Priority list. Choosing only few tasks will help you focus and really get them done.

Step 4

Step 4 is about being productive anywhere. Using your computer, smartphone or tablet. Today's era of technology enables us to get tasks done anywhere and have more free time later!

Here we'll focus on getting things done not only in your traditional work environment but also anywhere else... with your mobile smart phone or a tablet computer... or a piece of paper.

The strength of a real productivity system starts with its accessibility and being ready for you anytime, anywhere, anyhow. It's also important to have the information on your devices always in sync.

I'm sure you've already somehow embraced the concept of the cloud. The Internet cloud. Remember, productive people are not afraid of the cloud ;-)

This simply means, your data is securely stored on some distant server. All you do is take a device you have at hand like a computer, smartphone or tablet, and access this data.

This already happens with your email. It's stored on your computer as well as on a server somewhere. It is happening with your contacts if you sync them with Apple's or Google's or Microsoft's systems.

If you know tools like Dropbox or Evernote, these also store your files and notes in the cloud as well as on your computers and smartphones. It works like magic.

The benefits of keeping the data in the cloud are amazing - you can get to it from anywhere, with any device and this other 'cloud' company takes good care of the security infrastructure around your data.

I know it may sound kind of spooky, but on the other hand,

should your house burn down (or simply your computer equipment be stolen), your data will be safe. Up there in the cloud.

Cloud companies deal with hundreds of thousands to millions of users (like Evernote, Dropbox or us, Nozbe) and they know how to create their backup infrastructure to ensure your data is safe at all times. We live and breathe by this.

Of course, you can always print out your tasks, documents and notes. And if it's in the cloud, you can print those from any computer that's connected to the Internet as you log in to your service's online account.

Nozbe was born as a cloud service. Initially you could access Nozbe data using a desktop Internet browser. Later, to give you the best Nozbe experience on a smartphone - we have created a special "slimmed down" version of our web application called Mobile.Nozbe.com where you can get your tasks done on the move.

And to make the mobile experience even better, we've built native apps for the iPhone, iPad, Android and Windows Phone. These apps work offline - meaning even if you don't have an Internet connection, you can still get your tasks done and synchronize with the cloud later.

Again, making the "experience" better meant for us building native apps for the regular PCs, too. We've got apps for the Windows and Mac platforms - apps that also work without Internet connection and sync with the cloud later.

Traveling on the plane? On a train or bus? Sloppy or non-existent Internet connection? You'll get stuff done with Nozbe anyway because our native apps work totally offline and sync your data when possible.

I don't want this step to sound like a sales pitch - but to make my point - to be really productive you need to use solutions that work across all the platforms you use - that's why I use Evernote, Dropbox and Nozbe - and sync my contacts with Apple's iCloud service...

Why is this "cloud" and "sync" thing so important? Well, imagine yourself running errands with your mobile phone. In Nozbe you'd click on the "Errands" context and you'd know what you need to do or buy.

Shopping for stuff? You are buying stuff and checking them off the list from a project you share with your wife. Suddenly your wife remembers you need to buy something more - she adds it to your project and boom, the information is automagically pushed to your mobile device.

Waiting for comments on tasks from your colleagues while on your way to a very important business meeting? The new comments arrive quickly on your mobile device as it syncs itself with the cloud. You won't miss anything.

That's why it's so important to have the key data in the cloud - to ensure you can access it from anywhere and that it can be updated by your teammates or other people you work with.

Whatever solution you choose to help you get things done, make sure it works across all platforms, supports instant synchronization and delivers a great work experience on your device. You'll always have the tasks you should focus on without worrying about how they are stored and synced.

Step 5

Step 5 is about collaborating. We live in a connected world and your colleagues as well as your close friends can help you get a lot more done. You'll learn how to share projects, delegate tasks and communicate through them effectively.

Here we'll talk about how you can learn to work with other people and start to communicate through tasks to get things done.

Newsflash: Everyone's day equals 24 hours. You can't stretch it. You can't bend the time. And if you can, please tell me how, I really want to know! But for now, let's assume - it's impossible. Let's just face it :-)

Reality check: You can't do everything better than everyone. You're not always the right man for the job. In order to succeed you need to embrace the fact, that others can do a "good enough" job and help you succeed.

If you think explaining stuff to others is a waste of time, think again. It's an investment. Once they get the hang of it, they'll do an amazing job. You'll be surprised. And relieved :-)

What I'm saying is that even if you've mastered the previous lessons from our course, you have organized tasks into projects, chosen your next actions and you even work "on the move", the day still has only 24 hours for you.

The most successful people on the planet, Sir Richard Branson, Bill Gates, Warren Buffett, and many others... are not doing everything themselves. They get stuff done with others.

I'm not saying you should hire hoards of people, but get into habit of delegating tasks to others, work collaboratively and enjoy the benefits of a job done in a group.

So start small. Start with tiny tasks and small favors... ask your spouse, friend or colleague to do something for you, tell them why it's important to you. Offer to return the favor.

So how do you do that? How do you delegate tasks to others? How do you make sure they get them done? Let's dive into practical aspects of delegating.

You can go to someone and physically tell them to do something for you, you can call them if they are not in the same place as you are... or email them.

Well, talking to someone or calling them is nice and very social, but not very practical. First off, talking to someone might disturb them and interfere with their workflow... and second thing is that they might (and probably will) forget about what you just asked them to do.

Emailing a task is better. It's all neatly written in a message and they receive it in their inbox. But they might still forget it. Or be buried with email... and you can't track the task's progress.

And very often emailing back and forth about specifics of a task leads to more friction and more conversation about the given task than actually necessary.

That's why it's key to delegate tasks through some kind of a system. That's why we integrated "project sharing" and "task delegating" into Nozbe to help you create a habit of "communicating through tasks".

When you share a project with someone, you can create tasks for yourself and for them. Now you've got your "common space" to do things. Away from email and other distractions. But to make sure it works remember some key points:

Make task names as brief as possible. Communicate clearly. If a task needs more specifics, add these to the comments of the task. You can comment with your Evernote notes or Dropbox files if you need to.

You can comment with anything you want. Sometimes a document is needed, other times a short description, or an image or photo, or a short checklist. Nozbe makes commenting a breeze to ensure your message gets through.

When you delegate a task to someone, it automatically becomes their "Next Action" so you'll know they've received it. Then they'll proceed to this task while processing their Priority task list for the day.

Once the task is completed, it'll be included in your email report. And visible in the project. You'll be able to easily track the task and see if it needs more specifics before it's done.

Bottom line: once you get into the habit of working with others, you'll love it and you'll enjoy a synergy that's simply incredible. 1+1 usually equals more than 2 or even 3 if you're working with someone.

Communicate through tasks and get things done! You'll love it.

Step 6

Step 6 is about working in contexts - it's a second, and very helpful layer of productivity, where you divide tasks not only into projects, but into places these can be done in, tools these can be done with, and so on.

Here we'll talk about "Contexts" - a concept borrowed from the David Allen's book "Getting Things Done". In short "GTD".

Well, you already are a productivity ninja as you've mastered the way of adding tasks, organizing them into projects and getting them done from your "Priority" list.

Although I'm not a big fan of prioritizing, I like "categorizing" to-do lists thanks to a method from GTD called "contexts". The "Contexts" concept is another weapon to help you clear these lists and get more done.

As David Allen says - a Context can be a place, a tool or an environment.... which can be applied to various tasks in different projects.

Some examples for contexts: tools like "phone" (because you have to call people regarding various projects, right?)... Places like: Office or Home (because you can perform some tasks only there)... and "state" like "Writing" (to mark tasks that require extensive amount of writing).

Again, it's a way of categorizing tasks from different projects so that you can batch them and get them done together. Before we move on, let me explain the concept of "batching".

"Batching" means, grouping the same tasks that require the same skills, or effort, or tool, or environment... like when you cook - and first gather all the ingredients you need to slice and slice them, later all the ingredients you need to fry, and fry them... because doing slicing, then frying, then slicing would be counter-productive.

My other favorite example is the "phone" context. Imagine you've just had a lunch. It was great, you're stuffed and you're back at your desk and you don't feel like working... yet. Happens to me very often. What do I do to bring myself back into "action mode"?

I do something that doesn't require a lot of effort and is very rewarding. I start calling people up. I first call my wife to ask how she's doing and although I try to keep it brief - this makes her happy every time.

Then I click on the "Phone" context in my Nozbe app and the whole list of tasks I previously defined as "phone calls" pops up. I call these folks one by one and start feeling very productive. I'm getting things done despite being stuffed with food!

Another example: My CFO and I often need to make some payments. I also need to pay my landlord or car insurance or some other thing... I group all these into Finance context. This way I can batch my wire transfers even though they come from different projects.

A context can be a person: My wife has her "Boss" context and whenever she has a task that she wants to review with her boss, she marks it with "Boss" context. Later, when she is about to have a meeting with him, she prints all of her tasks from the Boss context and she knows exactly what to discuss during that meeting.

Other examples of contexts include "shopping", because you may need to buy groceries, but on your way back home it'd be great to pick up printer paper for your home office and a new set of pens.

I frequently use "Errands" as a context to run errands (small things I need to take care of or buy when running around town)... This is really helpful because otherwise I would forget about something from some project...

And if you're really into prioritizing, you can set up a "Top priority" context in Nozbe and mark with this context tasks that are really just your priority. The possibilities are endless.

Again, grouping tasks into contexts is not the same as grouping them into projects. In Projects you group tasks around a common goal while with Contexts you group around similar way of getting them done.

Contexts serve as an additional weapon as you can now group tasks from various projects together depending on their place, tool or environment... whatever suits you and helps you get things done.

In Nozbe you can quickly add new contexts to tasks. Just pull out the context list and drag and drop context on the tasks (or tasks on contexts) to assign one to another. And the contexts are being shared automatically when you share a project with other people!

Try it for yourself - choose a short list of contexts and see how they'll improve your productivity. Remember to use the same contexts across multiple projects and you'll see how it helps you move these projects forward.

The concept of Contexts will help you get things done and process many actions at a time when you're the most productive - with a tool at hand, in a certain environment or even with someone.

Step 7

Step 7 is about managing your reference material and documents. Store your notes and digitize as much content as you can to make sure to have it at hand when you're getting your tasks done. Lots of tricks and apps can help you with that.

Here we'll learn to deal with our "reference materials" - all the documents that are required to get certain tasks done.

Productive life starts and ends with to-do lists... but there is something in between - the reference material and all the helpful documents you need, to really get your tasks done.

Your documents, notes, files are not an integral part of your productivity system, but they are the "backbone" of information you need and they provide key insights that help you get a task done.

While I spend most of my day making sure the tasks get done, I would be lost without the remaining two parts of the puzzle - notes and files.

People deal with reference material in different ways, some use drawers where they put physical documents, others go "all digital" and scan everything to their computer.

While I appreciate the physical documents and I keep the originals at hand, I still prefer to move most of my stuff in digital form. It requires more effort (scanning) but it pays off.

It's the mobility thing - once you have stuff scanned to a cloud-based system, you can access it from anywhere even with a mobile phone (as we mentioned in step 5 about mobility)

There are great apps to help you go "all digital" and "all cloud" like Evernote or Dropbox. They have native apps on most of the platforms.

In Nozbe you can attach a note or file to any project as well, and access these from all of the devices, too. It's pretty powerful and very handy!

Now, the key to maximum productivity is having the "relevant reference material" next to their relevant projects so that when you're doing a task, you have the needed documents and files at hand.

It would be even better if you had relevant documents attached not only to a project, but also to a task. This way when you're getting a task done, you have all the information necessary right there.

That's where many simple to-do lists and paper-only lists might fail – because all you see is a task and nothing more... you don't have access to other relevant information...

OK, this info is not necessary most of the time for most of the tasks... but when you're trying to get a more complex task done, very often you'll lose precious time finding the documents needed to complete it.

That's why in many modern productivity apps, like Nozbe, the system is built in such a way that you can see the documentation right next to the tasks.

In Nozbe we even let you comment on a task with documents, files, short checklists, YouTube videos, hyperlinks, and more…

And when you're using external systems like Evernote or Dropbox… Nozbe can automatically search for relevant items there and show them to you right in your projects…

And Nozbe even lets you comment with Evernote or Dropbox files right next to a task you're planning to work on. This way, you're still using your favorite system for storing reference material…

You're then using it together with your favorite task management app. We designed it like this because we actually use these services ourselves.

The Key is to use the systems you're comfortable with for storing documents and use a task-management system that let's you quickly find the relevant information that will help you get things done.

Very well prepared tasks are important, but very often you need more info to get them done. You're much better off with a good reference material system that helps you show relevant information to your tasks. Make sure to set it up well at the beginning and reap the rewards in the end.

Step 8

Step 8 is about reviewing your recently set up productivity system. At least once a week you need to have a meeting with yourself and review your tasks, projects, lists and goals. Learn to start your next week fresh!

Here we'll make you schedule 1-2 hours a week for a meeting with yourself to review your productivity system. Trust me, it's a very important meeting.

So you have mastered the previous 7 steps of our system. You know how to clear your head, organize tasks into projects, define next actions, work from anywhere and with anyone... and use contexts and reference material.

That's great. But even if you've done all that and you feel like a Superhuman, you still might fall off that wagon very quickly... if you don't review it all regularly.

Productivity experts suggest you should schedule a regular, weekly meeting with yourself to review everything you've done and everything you're set out to do.

David Allen of GTD fame calls it a "Weekly Review" and he says it's the moment when he thinks ahead for a week... and he knows, he'll think again in a week or so... and he basically does stuff without thinking in between.

He's exaggerating but this weekly reunion with yourself is the key to a successful productivity system. This is where we cement our commitment to getting tasks done.

It's hard to keep this habit though. We're constantly busy and our time is in demand by many people. We hardly find 2 hours (and that's usually what it takes) to review our productivity system.

I sometimes fail at this myself. I sometimes decide "I know what I have to do more-less" so I skip my Weekly Meeting with myself. And I shouldn't. And you shouldn't, too.

I heard someone say at a conference I was attending that a "Weekly Review must be done at least once a month" and it may sound funny, but this is the maximum length of time you can allow yourself to go. More than a month and you're off the wagon.

First of all, make it a "scheduled meeting" and block off these two hours in your calendar every week. You can do it either on Friday or Monday ... or weekend. Just make it happen. It's just two hours (and very often even less than that).

Here's how my Weekly Review meeting looks in a nutshell: First I calm myself down (I'm Catholic so I pray for 5 minutes and thank the Lord for my wonderful life).

I clear all my physical inboxes - the one near my desk, the one in Nozbe, my email inbox (if it's not at zero at this moment), and any other incoming materials that I haven't processed.

I review my "strategy mind map" - I use mind mapping software to outline my "strategy" and my long term goals. I review those and see how I've performed.

I never put actionable items in my Mind Map - I focus on goals there and make relevant projects in Nozbe where I put my tasks and other specifics.

I review all of my projects in Nozbe - all of them - I click on them one-by-one and check the tasks there, reschedule, modify or remove them... or rearrange them to other projects.

Reviewing all of my projects takes a while (and I have around 50 at this moment) but it makes sure my system is current. Nozbe is a tool I use every day, it needs to be clean and ready, just like the rifle of a soldier.

I go back to my Mind map and check if I should add some projects or tasks to Nozbe, I set up my next actions for the week and add necessary comments to them if needed.

With all that in place, I pray again and thank the Lord for a great week and ask him for wisdom for the next week. If you're not a religious person, just meditate or listen to your favorite music.

That's it. The key is to do it consistently. To do it every week (or every other week - but no less than every month). This is a regular meeting with yourself. You need it.

Just like we meet with other people, we need to meet with

ourselves and review our productivity system on a regular basis to make sure it's current, ready and very, very actionable.

Step 9

Step 9 is about Email and how to handle it. How to process it to zero and how to handle others' expectations when it comes to an email reply. How to make sure you don't get lost in the flood of email messages coming in.

Here I'll share with you my best practices and tips when it comes to email. How I get email done every day. And how I integrate it with my productivity system.

One thing is your productivity tool and the one you choose can be Nozbe or any other tool that has most of the characteristics we mentioned in previous steps. Your tool should encourage you NOT to "organize tasks" but to really "get tasks done" and move forward to achieve your goals!

Now, the other tool most of us have to use every single day is Email - it's used by everyone. Most of us see more and more messages coming at us day in and day out. Here are some tips that might help you get the email chaos under control.

I'm a firm believer in "Inbox Zero" meaning I keep my email inbox at level zero every day. With every incoming email I decide what to do with it, whether it's actionable or not, if I should reply now or later, or just archive it.

When replying to email, I use a "2-minute rule" meaning, if I know I can reply in less than 2 minutes I do it right away. And as I increasingly process my email on my iPhone or iPad, I've learned to send away quick answers. Trust me, people prefer a quick answer than none at all.

Most of the better apps out there assign you a personal email address which you can use to add information to them. I use Evernote and Nozbe daily and I email myself tasks, articles and they are automatically added to these systems.

When processing email, these "email gates" really help a lot. When an email is actionable, I forward it to Nozbe, if it's a reference material, I forward it to Evernote. It's quick and I don't need to leave the email application to add a task or a note.

Another thing is that I no longer "check email". I "process email". I know, sounds similar but there's a big difference. When you process something, it's done, when you check something, it's still out there.

That's why I encourage you to turn off the "auto-checking" feature in your email client and turn off "push-email-notifications" in your smartphone. Every hour make a conscious decision to "process email" and deal with every email message there to clean your inbox to zero.

I know it sounds very drastic and you might think people want you to check email every minute of every hour of every day. Trust me, if you communicate the expectations, they will let you change this habit.

And this way you can get an hour (or more) of focused time when you are not being interrupted by the sound of an incoming email. When people know you get back to them, they'll let you do your job and respond to them a little later...

I actually go even more drastic with that. I don't check email until noon every day. I'm an early riser. In the morning it's my "creative time" and I only focus on the important tasks. It's my time.

Only at around noon or 1 PM I fire up my email client and process my email inbox to zero. It takes me around 30 minutes. This way I can respond to my peers and be a part of the team again.

From then on I process my email every hour or so. And it takes me a few minutes each time. At the end of the day I respond to some longer emails I needed to take care of.

You see, from checking email and letting it interrupt me I've gone to processing email at the times I feel are good for me and not for others. It helped me find time to focus on my creative work.

Another tip: when I do my creative work I use something called a "Pomodoro Technique". Meaning, I divide my day into many 25-minute chunks. I work for 25 minutes straight and then relax for 5 minutes.

This technique is really great and helps me stay focused. The clock is ticking, I know I have only 25 minutes to complete a task so I just go with it. You'd be surprised how much can be done in 25 uninterrupted minutes.

This technique also helps me "get back on the wagon" when I feel this is not my best day and I'm slacking off. I just decide on one task, put the timer on, and say "let's go" and amazingly I'm getting my productivity mojo back!

One more tip: how to start a day fresh and productive? Just write three tasks you need to get done first thing in the morning and put them next to your bed before you fall asleep. Your mind will work on these tasks when you sleep.

Let's summarize: this is how I handle email and my focused work. Prepare your day with three key tasks, process email to zero and work in 25-minute chunks and you'll be very productive. I encourage you to give it all a try.

Step 10

Step 10 is where I help you start with everything you've learned so far. I will add several tips and tricks that work for me and point you toward additional materials for inspiration for action.

Here I'll help you start putting your own productivity system in place. We've covered a lot of material in the past lessons, don't let it overwhelm you, let's go!

As we said, what's on your mind is what's bothering you, so make sure to put your thoughts, documents and everything else into one big inbox. Literally put them all in a box.

Now start processing the box until it's at zero. Decide what to do with a piece of paper. If it's actionable add to your task and project management system (like Nozbe), if it's reference material, put it in your drawer, or scan it to Evernote, Dropbox or Nozbe or somewhere else.

Decide on each and every element and move on. Keep on keeping on until the inbox is empty. Don't worry if after doing all this your productivity system is not perfect, you'll tweak it as you go. Congratulations, you've done your first step.

Now work with your system, add more tasks, move them around, create more projects, delete or reorder other ones. Work with all this for a week and see your first results.

Now, after the first week is gone, review everything. See what's in your inbox, review each project, clear things up, see where you can improve, what you can change.

Now, schedule your next week's review.

Keep this all up for the next 4 weeks. Make sure not to miss any weekly review session with yourself and keep on improving the system. Be religious about putting everything in your inbox, don't shove it anywhere else. What gets in the inbox, eventually gets taken care of.

In the meantime practice email processing. Archive all the emails in your inbox that are more than 1 month old. Process the rest one by one and decide what to do with them. After a few hours your Email inbox will be at ZERO. Congrats!

Communicate to your peers your new email strategy. Start small - tell them you will process Email every hour. Turn off all the "email sounds" - it's not nineties anymore - you're not THAT happy about an incoming email as you used to be.

Get inspired. Subscribe to some productivity blogs like: Lifehacker, Lifehack, my own blog and some more. Download latest issues of the Productive! Magazine. Make sure you get a nice feed of new information coming in every day to help you get inspired.

Read more - I'm not an avid reader by design but I understand the value of good books and I read about a book a week. How? I don't actually read them, people read them to me - I listen to audiobooks - and I've got plenty of time for it - in my car, when I jog, run errands, you name it. You'll be amazed how much time you spend on the move - use it.

Having said that, I do encourage you to read books by David Allen, Stephen Covey, Brian Tracy, Tony Robbins and the authors that publish regularly in the Productive! Magazine.

Find a "productivity partner" - someone who is also starting to build their productivity system. Work with them. Share your idea with tips and tricks to keep on improving your systems and to encourage one another.

Don't be afraid to experiment with many techniques like Pomodoro I mentioned earlier.

Learn to touch-type if you don't already. I know beginnings are hard and it feels like going back to primary school, but you'll type 2-3 times faster after a month of training. There are many courses on the Internet as well as programs for Macs and Windows.

Don't be a slave to your calendar - try to only put events there that must occur at a certain date and time. Leave out the rest. Don't depend on your calendar for planning so much. Your task system serves this purpose.

By the way, Nozbe syncs with Google Calendar so you'll be able to see your due dates of tasks in your Google Calendar and on your smartphone if you sync it all. If you prefer the "calendar view", there is a way to go.

Get a smartphone if you don't have one. Get Nozbe or other task management app there that syncs with your desktop. You'll be amazed how much can be done when you are on the move.

Congratulations for making it this far! I wish you all the success and if you have questions, find me on my web site: MichaelSliwinski.com or on Twitter and Facebook or simply email me at michael@nozbe.com.

5: STRESS BUSTING

More and more we are seeing an increase in the stress levels placed on us in our lives. For us to remain healthy and productive it is important to reduce it as much as possible.

When you are trying to deal with stress, the most important thing is to know what stress is. What is this psychological condition that has ensnared 9 in 10 people of the world to some extent or the other? It is only when you know stress can you make an effective plan to combat it.

In this chapter, we shall learn about the different definitions of stress, and then we will focus on the definition that is the most accurate to today's scenario. We will come up, close and personal will stress so that we realize how we can fight it.

What Is Stress

Stress has been defined in several different ways. Each definition has some kind of relevance, but we shall shortly speak about the definition that should matter to us the most.

A popular medical website defines stress as:-

"The physical and emotional strain which is caused by our response to the pressure from the outside world."

This definition is good, and seems correct. But there is something very important missing. Let's see some other definition and the missing element will become apparent.

The definition of stress according to the Merriam-Webster Dictionary is as follows:-

"The physical, chemical or emotional factor that causes bodily or mental tension and which may be a factor in the cause of disease."

Another definition forwarded by the same dictionary is:-

"The state resulting from stress, i.e. the state of bodily or mental tension which are a consequence of factors which purport to alter a prevailing equilibrium."

Both of these definitions again have the same element missing, and that makes them inadequate.

Oxford Dictionary defines stress as:-

"A state of mental or emotional strain which is a result of adverse or demanding circumstances."

Once again, this definition does not make us too happy. Let us look at some more definitions that a random search on the Internet threw up for us.

"Stress is a normal physical reaction to various events that can make people threatened or can upset their balance in some manner."

"Any factor that brings forth a threat or a challenge to our state of wellbeing is defined as stress."

"Stress is the condition where people feel that they have too much on their platter; when they feel overloaded and feel that they are not capable of facing the various challenges that they face."

With all these definitions, that one element that we were looking for still remains missing and so we can just pass them by.

Now, here are the definitions that I really like:-

"Stress is the response that the human body provides when it is met with circumstances that induce it to behave, alter or modify in some manner to maintain their comfortable state of balance."

"Stress is the body's way of reacting to a challenges and getting prepared to face with tough situations with concentration, determination and strength with a state of total alertness."

Did you realize already why I like the last two definitions and not the ones mentioned before? Here is what worked for me... and what should work for you as well.

With the previous definitions, the problem is that stress is defined just as the influence of outside negative factors on the body. These definitions consider the body as a latent object, which can be easily manipulated by outside forces. But, with the last two definitions, the big difference is that stress is called as a 'reaction' or a 'response'. These definitions consider the body as an actionable force; and it considers humans as beings who can do something about negative situations that they encounter in life.

Most people have the whole idea of stress pegged on wrong. They think that stress just happens and they can do nothing about it, except complain and brood. They think that they simply are meant to wallow in stress and do nothing about it.

That is hardly the case. The truth is that our bodies are very well capable of dealing with the negative situations that will inevitably crop up in our life. And it is these reactions that are termed as stress.

What we see here is the gross ignorance people have about stress. Maybe you have the completely wrong idea as well. You are thinking about 'being stressed' as a situation where you do nothing and are simply worried about the circumstances in your life. The truth is that 'being stressed' means being NOT DEFEATED from the various negative situations that present themselves in your life. Being stressed means fighting those challenges. Being stressed means coming up a winner whenever you indulge in these fights.

Factors that Create Stress

Now that you have a better idea of what stress is, it is a good time to understand what causes stress. What are these factors that should precipitate you into taking a particular action?

You may already have some idea about the things that can cause stress, but you should know that there are a lot more factors out there.

Stressors are not so simple that they can be slotted into a single category. In analogy with that, you can see that stressors aren't something that you can have a uniform fight with. Each of these factors have a different way of dealing with them.

But, first, let us get acquainted with these detractors that can pull us down in life.

Factors that Create Stress

It is a circle, really. First, there is something that causes grief and depression within us, but then we come out of our slumber and try to fight against that factor. Like in a game of chess, the factor first causes the stress in us and then the stress in us causes a reaction that gives the check and mate to the factor and eliminates it. We have to make sure to maintain that balance. We have to ensure that we can remove every stress-causing element in our life with the stress itself.

But, in order to be able to do that, we have to first identify what those factors are. What are these factors that can cause such specific reactions to happen within us?

On the whole, we can classify these stress-inducing factors are external stressors and internal stressors. Both are equally dangerous if they are left to be as they are. And both need to be fought against with equal fervor if we want to ensure a happier life for ourselves.

Let us see what these external and internal stressors are.

External Stressors

These are the changes happening in the environment around us that pose adverse situations for us. These things are happening in our external environment, and hence we call them as external stressors. When these changes happen, our body begins to react in a particular way. We get a feeling of being threatened.

External stressors can confront us anywhere. They may come up at work… a looming deadline is a good example. They may relate to financial matters. A bill that has to be paid, some payment that has not yet come, tax that is overcharged, a wrong credit card score, etc. are so many different things that can disorient your living.

There can also be such factors in relationships. In fact, most of the stress-inducing factors happen in relationships. This is because two people are involved… two people with two different ways of thinking. Things are definitely going to make noise when opinions clash.

There can be so many other kinds of external stressors. The current political situation could be a stress-causing factor for you. If your home needs to be renovated, it could cause stress even if you have money. Someone close to you leaves you and goes away. Again, that can cause a lot of stress.

Stress happens in joyful situations also. If there is a wedding in the family, the stress that is caused there is indescribable. Why just wedding, anything that you have to organize in your house can cause stress, even a small kitty party! Also, something like an impending pregnancy can cause stress. You are happy about the little one coming to live with you soon, but maybe the anticipation is taking its toll on you.

Now, you shouldn't think that you have to move out of the house to feel stressed. There are so many ways in which stress can meet you in your house itself. We have already pointed out some such factors above. Bills to be paid, pregnancy, etc. are stress-causing factors that happen in the home itself. Something in your house doesn't work when you want it too… that can cause stress as well.

At the same time, you shouldn't think that stress has to be caused by monumental, life-changing factors. There are so many trivial matters over which we can get so worked up. Don't some people get stressed just because children playing outside make too much noise? Or that the dogs bark so loudly?

Or that the vehicles honk incessantly outside their house, even if they really don't? Or simply that the water for their bath isn't hot enough? Or that they have missed their bus?

All these are external factors that can cause stress. The list is endless, but these examples are more than adequate to help you understand what they are like.

Internal Stressors

Some of the stress-causing factors come from within. Mostly these are the mental problems that we so often face in today's world. These may manifest themselves in the form of depression, insomnia, ADD, and even more physical forms such as allergies, nausea and vomiting and digestive disorders, etc.

Internal stressors are usually more difficult to handle because they are working inside the body. They are related to your constitution and have a medical ground. Chronic diseases can also cause internal stress. People who suffer from heart-related problems or diabetes, for instance, are usually under a large amount of internal stress. Usually, the stress due to these factors also becomes chronic.

But, the situation is not all that bleak. There is very little we can do about chronic ailments, but not all internal stressors are related to chronic problems. Some of these can be easily managed, and even completely eliminated.

A lot of internal stress stems from the way you look at yourself, or the way you deal with things. For instance, if you have high beliefs or hopes about something and then it doesn't go your way, it can lead to stress. The solution here would be not to expect anything irrationally.

If you cannot focus on your work, that is internal stress as well. You can solve that by improving your concentration and finding new ways to motivate yourself. Other forms of internal stress comes in the form of low self-esteem, low self-perception, lack of confidence and other similar personality traits.

Sometimes, too much of a good thing is also bad. Just as high expectations can lead to stress, perfectionism can also lead to stress.

If you always seek perfection in everything, especially to a point of obsession, then it is going to hurt you at one time or the other. At the same time, if you are too eager to please people, then that could be a big problem as well, because you are not going to be able to do that all the time.

If you have habits that are not quite accepted socially, then those could be a problem as well. For instance, if you try to put people on, or if you are dishonest with people, then sooner or later, this could cause your balance to get disturbed.

Some internal stressors are rooted in the past. These are very difficult to get rid of. A childhood-related phobia, for instance, is difficult to shake off. If you have had a bad childhood or an abusive relationship, then it could leave a scar on you for a long time, and could become an internal stressor as well. Also, the habit of worrying too much, which could also have its origins in your past, can cause stress.

These are the various factors that can lead you to stress. Most of them are possible to control, though the going may not always be easy. You have to take stock of the situation. As we shall see in further chapters, you have to first come out of denial if you want to conquer your stress.

Your body will react to stress-causing factors in different ways. What you have to do is to channelize this response of your body so that it brings about positive results for you.

You have to target the response so that it eliminates the stress-causing factor.

Whether externally or internally produced, it is possible to combat stress, however difficult. It all starts with how much in acceptance you are, and then depends on how much effort you want to put in.

Signals that Tell You Are Stressed

One of the most deterring factors in any stress solution is that the person suffering from stress is in denial. They don't accept that they are going through any stress. Due to that, they do not want to react. This keeps them from finding the right respite for their problem and the problem keeps on aggravating.

Since we are talking about conquering your stress here, one of the most crucial things that you have to keep in mind is that you have to come out of your denial. You have to understand the fact that there are situations that are disorienting you, and only then can you start to think what you can do about them.

Understanding the stress signals is a very vital aspect of the stress-busting game. If you want your stress to react in the right manner, i.e. to remove the stressor, then first you have to know that you are stressed. Here are the signals that you have watch out for.

The most significant aspect of combatting stress is that you have to accept it. A lot of people, such as people who have a medieval idea of masochism, will probably hide the fact that they are stressed. Or, there are people who think that if they speak about their stress, their near and dear ones will begin to worry. There are also those obstinate people who believe that they can do everything needed to eliminate their stress factor all by themselves and hence they do not think they need to tell anyone about it.

Whatever be the situation, keeping your stress to yourself is highly counterproductive. Not only are you not going to come out of your stressful situation, but you are actually going to aggravate it.

To understand what you can do to remove your stress, the first and most important thing is to accept that you are stressed. You can do this by looking out for the signals. Are any of the following things happening to you?

Here, we are going to classify the stress signals as indicators of short-term and long-term stress. Short-term signals of stress usually manifest themselves when the stress-causing factor has been recent, or if something has happened recently that has aggravated the factor. Long-term stress is chronic. This happens mostly due to internal stressors, though even external stressors that have tormented you for a long time can cause such responses.

Signals of Short-Term Stress

The following is a list of the bodily symptoms of short-term stress.

➢ Your heartbeat becomes quicker.

➢ You sweat more profusely.

➢ You experience sweat on the palms of your hands and the undersides of your feet. There is also a cold sensation there.

➢ You find different sets of muscles in your body suddenly go tight despite your attempts to control them.

➢ Your breath becomes heavier.

➢ Your mouth runs drier.

➢ You have a sick feeling in the stomach.

➢ You have to go to the bathroom repeatedly.

➢ Things like muscular spasms, extreme fatigue, headaches and shortness of breath happen to you.

Here are some ways in which short-term stress can affect your productivity.

➢ You are not able to think clearly.

➢ You find it difficult to make choices.

➢ You find it difficult to build strategies.

➢ You become disinterested in things that previously used to interest you.

➢ You feel guilty about entertaining yourself.

➢ You feel bad about the simplest and the most necessary things in life too; like, you may want feel bad about eating your food.

➢ You become either very dejected or very short-tempered.

➢ You feel worried when you laugh.

If any of these signs start appearing, then it means that you are facing some stressful situation. But, that situation is definitely solvable; only you have to put in the right efforts once you have detected what it is.

Signals of Long-Term Stress

The signs of long-term stress are often quite radical. You need to be more worried about them, because it is possible that you have long forgotten what caused the stress in the first place.

People suffering from long-terms are usually prone to the following signs and signals:-

➢ Several of your habits change. This refers mainly to food and sleep. If you are eating differently than before, or sleeping in any way that is different, then it might mean that you are suffering from some kind of stress, which may not be quite apparent at that moment.

➤ Mood changes happen within you. You feel disoriented and confused. You act in a very emotionally-driven manner.

➤ Vices take hold of you. You start smoking and alcoholism, maybe even drugs.

➤ You neglect work and relationships, and spend more time doing nothing.

➤ You become careless of your looks.

➤ You become uncaring for the people around you.

➤ You talk more gloomy things as the days pass by.

These signals indicate that there is some long-standing stress within you. Something has snapped, and you have to take stock of the situation as soon as you can.

Stress Can Be Worked Out

If you have been following this chapter so far, then you will have understood one very important point… you can use your stress to eliminate your stress.

Take the stress constructively and then react positively in order to remove the stress. This is the approach that works. And, the one thing that you have to keep in mind is that it is always possible to eliminate the stressful condition.

However difficult it may seem, stress can never be permanent. This is not just positive thinking; it is a fact. You can become the master of your stress.

One of the most important things we have mentioned—which is also the most unorthodox concept present in this chapter—is that stress can be used to kill stress.

To reiterate… when a stressful condition presents itself before you, it is going to trigger some kind of response in you. You are definitely going to react. Now, most people react negatively when they are faced with a stressful situation. However, you should learn how NOT to do that. Instead of behaving negatively and succumbing to all those unappealing indications I previously, you have to channelize all your energies and try to remove the stress itself. You have to work in such a way that your stress is removed, and you can do that by directing your stress-influenced response in the right manner.

This chapter attempts to tell you what these methods are; how this can be done. You do not need any special tools or implements for that. You can do it just by making minor adjustments in your personality and in your way of thinking. Once you have these pat down, you will almost see your stress melting away.

Stress is a response of hormones within the body. It is hormones that create all kinds of sensations within us. Instead of allowing these hormones to react negatively and take us into the abyss of depression, we should focus these hormones to react positively. It is within us to build this high amount of enthusiasm and positive energy within us, energy that can move mountains!

So, the most important thing for you to keep in mind at this juncture is that stress is something quite transient. Do not make it a mainstay in your life. Target your stress-induced responses towards the removal of the factors that caused stress. And, keep your hopes switched on at all times. Be optimistic. That works like a shot in the arm when the going gets tough!

Here are some things that you have to pay attention to.

1. All kinds of stress can be worked out.

2. You need to have the determination to do it.

3. The way you begin is to first come out of the denial.

4. Then, think about the factor that has caused you the stress in the first place.

5. Sit down and think some more. What can you do in order to resolve that factor?

6. How will eliminating the stress-causing factor help you? This anticipation is often a great tequila shot for your efforts in eliminating your stress.

7. Work towards it. You cannot remove stress without putting in some effort.

Tips to Work Stress Out from Your Life

Let the action begin then. We have come a long way in understanding what stress really is, and now is the time to start learning what we can do about it. How can we become victorious against the demons of stress? Let's see some intelligent tips as to how that could be done.

Getting right to the topic, here we are going to speak about some methods in which you can work the stress out from your life. Implementing these tips would give a new lease to your life. Not only would you be able to work the current stress out, but following a lifestyle that is peppered with these suggestions can prevent future stressors from disorienting your life.

Breathe

When you are stressed, you are prone to feel a lack of blood circulation in the vital parts of the body, such as your brain. This is what hinders positive responses from your body. To counter that, deep breathing exercises can work fantastically. Sit down, and inhale deeply. Let the air go all the way down, right to the lungs.

You will feel better. As soon as the air enters those tiny cells of the lungs, it is exchanged into the blood and blood begins flowing with greater vigor. There is more blood supply to the brain and you feel more relaxed. Try out various breathing exercises; there is solid scientific rationale behind them.

Accept the Stress

A lot of people find a stressful situation more daunting because they are not willing to speak up. You need to sit down and accept that you are stressed. This is a very important first step in eliminating the factor that is causing you to be in turmoil.

Speak with People You Trust

Once you have admitted to yourself that you are stressed, the next step is to open out to your near and dear ones. Who is the one you trust the most? Tell them your problems. You will find that sharing your problem always makes it lighter. Even if the person cannot solve the problem for you, the simple fact that someone else knows about it helps you be at ease.

Seek Your Fun and Relaxation

Though a short-term solution, finding ways and means to relax and have fun can be highly effective. Involve yourself in some activity that you like to do. Spend time with your hobby. If you like watching movies, do it. If you would rather curl up with a book, do that. Maybe a little bit of traveling or even a small vacation can help you. If this is what you need, do it. Nothing is worth staying stressed for.

Go on a Nostalgia Trip

Most times, it really helps just to look at some past photographs or videos. Look at some of these memories of your past successes or look at some party pictures or the pictures of a holiday that you had. Such things can perk you up immensely.

When you see yourself enjoying with close people, the stress just seems to melt away. In fact, a lot of people get inspired when they look at such pictures. They become more cheerful and are able to think more rationally.

Exercise

Exercising is a very constructive way of beating stress. Hit the gym whenever you are stressed. In fact, if you make this a regular habit, you will find that the external as well as internal stressors do not affect you that much. Also, there is the very big advantage that you are making your body fitter. A fitter body houses a healthier mind as well.

Do Not Lose the Humor

Even if the going is tough, it does not mean that you should become all grumpy and grouchy. Do not forget how to laugh. Watch some good comedy shows or read some funny books or just hang around with your friends who like to live with a light mood. These things can perk you up immensely. If you forget how to laugh, the stress could eat you from within.

Do Not Entertain Negative Thoughts

Stress may induce thoughts such as jealousy, hatred, feeling of vengeance, a general low feeling and so on. You should avoid these thoughts at all costs. Remember that this is just a transient phase; it will soon pass away. There is no need for spoiling your way of thinking over it.

Pamper Yourself

It is a good idea to pamper yourself when you are stressed. Go to the salon and get some treatment that you would like to have. Get a massage if that's what you like. You will find these are great stress-busters.

Do Not Over-expect

A lot of stress comes from the fact that we tend to over-expect. We think too much about what we could get and then we let those feelings rule us. This should not happen. You should not build irrationally high expectations. Things will take their course, and you will get what you deserve. If you learn not to expect higher than what you deserve, then you can live a happier, stress-free life.

Dealing With Stress At Work

7 in 10 people who have jobs claim that their work is causing them stress. This may be your situation as well. Maybe your job is what is giving you something more than just your livelihood… it is also giving you the stress to live with. If this is happening, you are not alone.

But at the same time, there are things you can do in order to combat workplace stress. All of these things are quite doable. It is all in planning the right way and avoiding the negatives.

Workplace stress is one of the most common forms of stress. In today's times, it is very difficult not to carry some work back home. People are usually inundated with work, and that causes a great deal of stress to them.

In order to cope with your workplace stress, you need to first accept that your job is the cause of your stress. It is only when you come out of your denial can you overcome this form of stress; something that is true for every kind of stress that you might face.

Here are some tips you can use to deal with stress at the workplace.

1.   Take only as much work as you can do. For a lot of people, the stress is because they take up a lot of work, work that they cannot do. Promotions and incentives notwithstanding, the one thing that is very important to you is your health. You should know what your limit is, and then you should work within that limit. This is a very important point. If you just give your nod to work that you can realistically do, then you will be much happier about your job.

2.   Accept work with realistic and practicable deadlines only. Many people accept work with difficult deadlines just because of the lure of money or because of the fear of losing a client. But, if you are good at your work, you can always ask for more time to do your work. No work needs to be unrealistically chased. At least, not at the

cost of your health. When you take up work that you can easily do, then you are not only preventing stress from sapping your innards, but you are also able to provide better quality work to your clients.

3. Learn to say no. Most people cannot do that. Workplace stress actually stems from the fact that people don't know how to say no. When you cannot refuse, you end up taking things you cannot do. You take more work than you can handle, you accept unrealistic deadlines, you agree to help out your friends with things that they are supposed to do, you agree to do tasks for the company which you need not (such as organizing parties) and so on. There is no harm in doing all of this if you are capable of doing it. But, most people do not have that kind of powerhouse capacity. If you have to take up a lot of work and eventually it is going to cause you an immense deal of stress, then it is certainly not worth creating that impression of the 'guy or gal who can do it all'.

4. Manage your time. This is one of the most important things that anyone should learn, whether they have a job or not. When you are in a job, this becomes all the more important. When you learn how to manage your time, then you are able to fulfill your tasks in a much better way, with enough time left over for fun and recreation as well.

5. You have to absolutely learn how to prioritize things. This is extremely important. When you are able to fulfill tasks according to their order of importance, then you find the situation much easier to handle. One way of prioritizing things is by deciding which of your tasks can help the faster accomplishment of another task. If there is a particular task that should be done earlier so that the next task becomes easier, then follow that logical order.

6. Learn about new technologies all the time. You will be amazed to see the kind of progress that technology is making right now. This is the world of automation; there is a simple software solution for almost anything. Keep updated. There are chances that you could use some new technological solution to make your job easier. At the same time, when you are better informed, you simply know how to get your job done faster.

7.   Trust in your team. So many people build up a great deal of workplace stress just because they do not believe in the people around them. Give them their due importance. You should know that these people have also been employed by the same organization that has employed you, so you need to have at least some amount of faith in their judgment. If there is some task that someone else should do, let them do it. Do not insist on taking it up just because you feel you can do a better job. The whole thing could actually backfire. You may not be able to finish that and your work would be left in limbo as well.

8.   Keep time for your family and friends. Never immerse yourself in your work. Always remember that you are working for your family and yourself. Hence, give them due importance. Refrain from working on holidays and the weekends. Spend time with the family. Go out with your friends whenever you can. All these things really matter because they take your mind off work. When you revisit your work after such brief sojourns, you find that you can attack it with renewed vigor.

9.   Live a healthy lifestyle. Take care of your health. Go for a jog early morning, or at least get a treadmill. Leave only after having a healthy breakfast. Learning a good meditation technique such as Yoga is also not a bad idea. Do not drink and smoke just because you are stressed at work. These can only give you a temporary boost. When their effect wears off, you will be feeling more despondent than ever. Avoid calorie-rich junk foods and pile up on those veggies instead. Have fresh fruit juice instead of coffee at work. Sip water throughout the day; it helps keep your metabolism in a good working condition.

10.   Celebrate when you should, and don't just celebrate with your work people. If you have achieved some kind of victory at work, treat your family and friends. This gives you a sense of self-satisfaction. When you see your near and dear ones sharing in your victory, you feel that your achievement is not in vain. This also acts as a great motivating factor and you are able to tackle your next job with better enthusiasm.

Keep these points in mind. Workplace stress is sapping

everyone's mind at the moment, but you need to keep this demon away. Like with every other kind of stress, you should learn how to use the influence of stressors on your mind to bring about creative solutions. Do that, and workplace stress will become history for you!

Stress comes in various forms, but it is up to us to recognize it and deal with it in the right manner. Throughout this chapter, I have laid emphasis on how you should not be fazed by stress. Instead, you should take it constructively and use its influence to deal with the factor that caused the stress in the first place.

Stress can happen due to internal as well as external factors. Anything and anyplace could be a causative factor of stress. It can happen at work, it can happen in a relationship, it can also happen when you are sitting at home, doing nothing.

You have to keep that in mind. You have to realize that the monster of stress will come in various forms and you will have to counter it at that moment.

This chapter has given several ideas on how you can do that. But, what you should really take from this eBook are the various methods that help you lead a stress-free life forever. Improving your lifestyle is important; but you should pay attention to your health as well, especially your mental health.

So, stress isn't all that it is cracked up to be. It is present in the world outside, and we have to tackle with it in the right manner.

The best thing is that... We can deal with stress!!!

All it takes is the right knowledge and the right motivation to come out victorious from your stressful situation.

6: WHAT IN THE WORLD IS UNLIMITED ENERGY

As a person our can never run out of energy, our bodies are designed as machines and these machines run on energy, the energy we need comes from the food we eat but apart from that we can get our energy from the reserves stored in our body as fat. Our body stores excess energy as fat and we can transform the fat back into energy by using it up.

The Basics

We have unlimited energy because when our body energy is running low we can fuel up again and keep going. All energy comes from the ground, the food we eat comes from the plants we grow and these plants require minerals and nutrients from the ground. Even the meat that we eat requires the plants from the ground to sustain them. Energy is never lost but it is used up and transformed from different types.

Energy has many sources and when one source runs out then we can turn to alternative sources of energy. We can use this energy to make our lives more comfortable and we can even use this energy to better our lives.

If you are particularly feeling overweight instead of seeing yourself as fat you can see yourself as stored energy and to lose the weight you have to utilize the stored amount of energy.

The world has unlimited energy because it has many sources of energy and as we use the available sources we are creating new sources called bio energy. Bio energy is made from plants and animal fat and it solidifies in the ground as coal and this will be used later on as energy by other generations. This is a perfect example of why energy is unlimited.

Evaluate Where You Are Physically

It is important to know the status of your body, its physical condition and its level of fitness. Knowing the physical condition is important because you will be able to deal with foreseen problems and handle them before they become life threatening. Your body is a machine and knowing the condition of the machine will give you knowledge of when it needs to rest and not be overworked or when it needs repairs.

What Can You Do

Your body like any other machine needs to be fed the right type of fuel and oils to make it run properly, this means you need to find out what your body lacks in terms of minerals and try to give it the right kind of food. A better body means better health and better health leads to a better lifestyle. If your body is healthy you are most likely to be happier.

Going to the doctor to get a physical is the best way to evaluate the physical state of your body. You will be able to know if you are healthy or you need to either gain or lose weight, the level of your blood pressure, cholesterol levels and if you are lacking anything that your body needs.

It is important to know the state of the physical being internally because this might actually save your life and being smaller as a person does not necessarily mean that you are healthy you may have certain problems that you need to fix and you might actually be too small to be healthy.

It is advisable for everyone to get a physical examination with their doctor at least once a year and for males to have male related exams and females have female related exams. Implementing this into your lifestyle will keep you healthy and aware of what is happening inside your body not just what is happening on the outside.

Restore Your Metabolism

The word metabolism is derived from the Greek language. And it means "change" or "transformation". For our purposes of body function, metabolism is the amount of energy or calories your body burns to maintain vital bodily functions.

At every moment, be it that you are sleeping, or at the mall shopping or in the gym exercising, your body is constantly burning calories. It needs fuel just as a car needs fuel to power itself or a machine. Your metabolism is the regulator and manager of your body's fuel.

Certain type of foods may be eaten to boost the metabolic rate of the body. Food like whole grains, dark leafy greens and lean meat like fish and chicken are good for boosting the metabolism.

The time at which you eat is also important if you want to boost your metabolism. Eating frequent small low fat meals will work towards increasing your metabolism rate.

Staying long hours without eating slows down your metabolism that is why you start feeling weak and drained and craving for sugar because your blood sugar will be low.

Staying for a long period of time without eating makes your body feel as though you might be lacking food so it starts processing your food slowly in your digestive system as a way to preserve the food till you get more but if your body senses that you have adequate food it will process it faster and this will also avoid indigestion.

Drinking herbal tea and a lot of water also improves the metabolism rate. Water helps in digestion and distribution of nutrients in the body. Exercising is another way of boosting your metabolism, when you exercise your body will burn more calories in the following days that if you had not exercised and exercising in the evening is better than in the morning because that is when your metabolism is slowing down and this gives it a boost and you burn more calories throughout the night.

The Importance Of Energy Foods

Carbohydrates are energy giving food they are broken down by the body into the simple sugar glucose, which is used to give energy or will be stored for a short time in muscles and liver in the form of glycogen or animal starch.

The hormone insulin is vital for the oxidation of glucose the process of yielding energy for the body. When not enough insulin is generated and this may lead to diabetes.

Starches should be in your carbohydrate intake. The best sources of starches are bread, oats, rice and beans. Energy foods are important because they help you keep going throughout the day by supplying you with energy without these energy food we would feel weak and start craving for sugar that is when we start eating the wrong types of starch like cakes and biscuits that will make us fat.

Good fats are another way of getting the energy the body needs and these are important because they burn more slowly and keep the body going over a long period of time.

Without energy foods the body will stop functioning properly and some of its bodily functions will start shutting down, you will not be able to concentrate properly at work or in school and you will feel weak in some cases resulting in feeling faint headed.

Although we have to have these energy foods to keep our bodies running it is also important to make sure we take them in the right quantities because if too much is ingested then that will result in the excess energy being stored in the body as fat and if this continues to take place it leads to obesity and that opens up the body to many other diseases such as diabetes, stroke and high blood pressure.

Cut Down Stress

Stress comes from many areas in our lives and sometimes, it may be coming from areas that we are not even aware of. It could contribute to high blood pressure and heart attack and it can affect the way in which we perform our jobs or how we perform in school.

There changes we can implement in our lives to cut down on the stress, taking things a little lightly may help us in not getting stressed about what we are going through or what is happening in our lives that may be beyond our control. Avoiding isolation and being around family and friends will help us deal with things better and not have to face challenges in life alone.

Time management of all the things we have to do help us not be under pressure which further leads to stress. We need to make sure we do not put off things that we have to get done and rather face them head one and get them out of the way so they do not stress us in the near future.

In some cases people are stressed because they are assuming things about the unknown, assuming the worst may stress a person out. Stop assuming the worst and be hopeful for the best or merely wait for the outcome because obsessing about something you have no control over will definitely stress you.

Setting realistic goals that are (SMART) will avoid situations of being under pressure and stressed. Smart goals are specific, measurable, attainable, realistic and timely.

They are goals that are achievable not ones that will have you sweating out because you cannot reach them.

Sometimes, it is to our advantage for us to take a few hours just to relax. We live in a world that tells us that we have to keep going if we want to accomplish our goals; nevertheless, occasionally it is best to take a few uninterrupted hours just to relax. Relaxing is necessary once in a while.

Get Better Sleep

We are always told that sleep is important. There is great emphasis on the effects of losing sleep because losing sleep is certainly not something to be taken lightly.

An occasional night of tossing and turning is normal, but continued patterns of this behavior can cause real problems in your ability to function normally. Research shows that inadequate sleep can have disastrous effects on your weight loss efforts, impair your concentration, and even mimic the symptoms of impaired glucose tolerance (which can lead to diabetes and hypertension).

People that do not sleep well are usually grumpy and angry that is because your mood also suffers when you don't get enough shut-eye, causing you to become disoriented on the job, fatigued behind the wheel of a car, or irritated at home. Some people even start hallucinating because of lack of sleep. But more importantly, these mood swings can affect your relationships with others, and even lead to depression.

You can improve the quality and quantity of your sleep by implementing certain changes can make you sleep better. Get yourself into a routine. Try going to bed a half an hour earlier each week, or set a time to get in bed and stick with it. Eventually your body will get used to going to sleep at that time and it will begin to come naturally. Create the right environment. Get your body and mind in the habit of using your bedroom for sleeping. If you frequently sit in bed to pay your bills, do your homework, watch television, eat, talk on the phone, your mind will expect that the bedroom is for daytime activities.

Limiting food and activities before bed will help you fall asleep faster, having an activity to do before bed may make you more alert and slowing the process of falling asleep.

Why You Have To Exercise For Energy

Most people usually feel tired throughout the day, especially after lunchtime they feel sleepy and would rather stay indoors and watch television for the rest of the day.

Get Moving

Exercise is a great way to increase your energy level and fight off feelings of fatigue. A few minutes of daily exercise can really transform how you feel and also how much energy you have towards getting through your day.

Research shows that even among people with chronic illness like cancer or heart disease, exercise can ward off feelings of fatigue and help people feel more energized.

Studies have shown that people who exercise for a minimum of an hour a week divided into two 20 minute sessions per day have more energy levels to take them throughout the day than people who do not exercise at all.

The trick is exercising when you feel fatigued. Tired people generally do not want to put on their sneakers and go for a run. They can come up with all kinds of excuses of why they cannot go and exercise at that very moment.

The good news is that even a little bit of increased activity seems to be helpful. Jus increasing your heart rate up for a few minutes can getting you feeling better and further research proves that a few minutes of exercise a day and help you fight off stress.

When trying to exercise for more energy, the hardest thing to do is schedule the time. Choose a consistent time that you can exercise daily (like first thing in the morning, just before lunch or when you get home from work).

Make your goal to exercise at least 4 days a week and never go more than 1 day without exercising. It becomes harder to go back to your routine if you spend more time away from it. That way, you'll never get out of the habit of exercising.

The Importance Of Spiritual Connection

Most people do not realize that they need spiritual connection until they have all that they think they need but still they feel as though something is missing.

Most people feel a little more money may solve all their problems and some think marriage or a relationship will end their loneliness but after acquiring all that they have they still feel empty and that is when they realize that they need spiritual connection.

A human being will never be fully satisfied unless they have the feeling of a spiritual being that is far greater or higher that they are and that is God.

There's no denying it, when we feel connected and balanced spiritually we feel better physically and emotionally. Everything seems to be going well and we are able to deal with any situation that comes our way.

Nourishing the soul is as important as food, water and exercise. Some people claim to experience complete healing from certain health conditions through a variety of spiritual methods. Spiritual connection has so many benefits, when your spirit is healthy your body is healthy.

However, even if complete healing is not attainable, our physical health and overall sense of well-being can be greatly enhanced by enriching our spiritual health.

Your spiritual health as well as your emotional and physical health may be improved by cultivating more humor and gratitude in your life. They say laughter is the best medicine. Scientific research proves that even a fake chuckle is able to release toxins and chemicals into your body to help you relax.

Remembering to appreciate the simple things in life and not taking yourself too seriously. Most people beat themselves up and forget that life is to be enjoyed and the best way to do that is not taking for granted the smallest of things in life and embracing the nature around us.

Changing Your Emotions Changes Energy

When we are emotionally distressed the first instinct is to curl up into a ball and cry ourselves to sleep. Our emotions have an effect on our energy levels.

When happy we are able to jump around and up and about all day but when sad or angry we do not feel like doing anything at all we just desire that the day pass us by and not do anything.

This shows us that our emotions can change the amount of energy we have. Trying to maintain a stable emotions and not being annoyed or angry will help boost up the energy levels, maintaining a cheerful attitude will help you get through your day rather than sulking all day.

Remaining calm when a situation arises may help us in controlling our emotions, usually when something happens we are quick to panic and lose control sending us into an anger frenzy.

Being more accepting of a condition situation or even a person may help us with balancing our emotions. It is important to identify how to balance our emotions because when in control of our emotions then we are subconsciously in control of our energy levels.

Always finding time to yourself throughout the day will give you an opportunity to ask yourself if you are okay and if you are dealing well with all the different things happening in your life.

Alone time is very important that way you get to have your spiritual time and are able to relax and let go off all the stress from the long day you had. This helps you as a person to know that you are okay that you are in control and that you do not have to let your emotions take over and always remember if you are able to balance your emotions already you are working towards being happier meaning you will have more energy.

Why Being Energy Depleted Gets You Nowhere

That feeling you get of being drained and exhausted and as

though you cannot go on any more usually leads to feelings of self-resentment and furthermore anger.

Being energy depleted will slow you down and hinder you from having a good productive lifestyle because all you will do is sit at home and not do anything you will feel so sorry for yourself and you will not be interested in anything or even anyone.

This will lead to isolation and maybe even depression. It is important that you maintain positive energy in your life.

It is possible that if you lead a slow and boring lifestyle your friends will find you boring and you will realize that you are not invited to a baby shower or a barbeque and you will be asking yourself why you were left out, maybe it is because you drain the life out of a party or gathering.

Maintaining a positive attitude will also rub off your friends and colleagues and they will be motivated to be like you and that will help you in overall because you will always be surrounded by active lively and bubbly people.

At work being active and alert will convince your boss more that he needs you on the board or even in the leadership committee because of your lively and attentive personality.

There are endless reasons in how your energy in your life may affect you positively and gain you more advantages than if you were lifeless and drained.

No one wants to hang around the lifeless person who never wants to do anything or go anywhere and you cannot affect people positively in your life if you yourself are lifeless and in need of positive attitude.

7: CONCLUSION

I hope that you have enjoyed this book and have learned tips, methods and techniques that you can put into action to not just make you productive but to turn you into a super star.

Having the right tools and systems in place and knowing how to use them makes the difference. You now have the tools you need and I have also spoken about reducing stress, getting motivated and how to raise your energy levels to maintain your productivity.

If you would like to continue learning, I offer training workshops, group coaching, one-on-one coaching, masterminds and corporate training.

Not only do I offer training on productivity but I also offer coaching on business systems and branding.

Thank you for reading this book and joining me on the journey to success.

www.ingramcontent.com/pod-product-compliance
Lightning Source LLC
Chambersburg PA
CBHW051328170526

45166CB00002B/732